Dodie Bellamy is a national treasure. (I'll go further: Dodie Bellamy is an international treasure.) Her sentences—like water from a prelapsarian spring—have amazing purity and tonal accuracy; they hold themselves accountable to the highest standards of candor. In *The TV Sutras* she is in top form, hilarious and enlightening as an anarchist bodhisattva moonlighting as a performance artist. I gorge on Bellamy's genius.

—WAYNE KOESTENBAUM

Part porno, part memoir (maybe), part spiritual teaching (probably not), part fiction, *The TV Sutras* is a page turner. Bellamy's writing is, line by line, literally exciting, driving, flowing, churning, so disarmingly, so sincerely, confessional, it's got to be fake, and probably is, but you can't tell it's so hyper-believable—and so serious in its love for and skepticism about zany and banal spiritual teachings and the cults that convey them. Her writing about the sexual energies that swirl around the guru figure—from the point of view of a woman thrilled by them—is all too convincing. By the time you get to the transcendent final page it hits you that you have always been in a cult of one sort or another—and that you are god.

—NORMAN FISCHER

THE TV SUTRAS

The TV SUTRAS

Dodie Bellamy

UGLY DUCKLING PRESSE :: DOSSIER

The TV Sutras
© 2014 by Dodie Bellamy

ISBN 978-1-937021-39-1

Distributed to the trade by
SPD / Small Press Distribution
spdbooks.org

First Edition, First Printing
Printed and bound at McNaughton & Gunn
Designed by goodutopian
Illustrations and cover art by Neil LeDoux

Ugly Duckling Presse
The Old American Can Factory
232 Third Street #E-303
Brooklyn, NY 11215

Funded in part by a grant from
the National Endowment for the Arts

NATIONAL
ENDOWMENT
FOR THE ARTS

uglyducklingpresse.org

You don't need me to tell you
that it all might be an hallucination

or some sort of Light Show of the Gods

I mean, take another look at
the 9th book of Plato's *Republic*

Or you might say that even the
concept of "home" is risible

Maybe all of us have to sing a blues tune
from nursery to nursing:

"Delude me, baby
Delude me, all night long!"

—Ed Sanders

TV SUTRAS

Truth is a pathless land.
—Krishnamurti

THE SOURCE OF THE TRANSMISSION

As soon as I sit down to meditate a car alarm goes off, a loud insistent EEHHH EEHHH EEHHH EEHHH EEHHH. I get up from the living room floor and walk to the back of the apartment to see if it's quieter. The EEHHH EEHHH EEHHH EEHHH EEHHH is even louder. There's no escaping it. I either have to meditate through it or give up. So I sit down again in the hellish noise and focus on my breathing. *The TV Sutras* is an inspired text born from a crisis of urban bombardment.

I use "inspired" in the spiritual sense, meaning a text that is dictated or revealed. For example, each day between noon and 1 p.m., Aiwass, the minister of Horus, dictated *The Book of the Law* to Aleister Crowley in the spring of 1904. And then there's Moses, who climbed Mount Sinai so God could dictate the Ten Commandments to him. For *The Urantia Book,* space aliens spoke through a sleeping man named Wilfred Kellogg in Chicago, Illinois, USA. For the *Book of Mormon,* Joseph Smith dropped a magical seer stone into his hat, then buried his face in the hat, and in the darkness a spiritual light shone, revealing a parchment. On that parchment strange writing appeared, one character at a time, and under it, conveniently, was the English translation. At Delphi, the priest would seat an illiterate woman on a great bronze tripod over a vaporous crack in the ground. The woman would chew laurel leaves and enter a trance. From her incoherent babbling the priest would interpret sacred messages. Stories abound of people who crouched in caves, climbed craggy cliffs, dragged their asses through the desert, roughed it in the wilderness, starved, sweated, flagellated themselves, drank brews that made them retch, smoked weed, dug through animal entrails to receive inspiration from the beyond.

In receiving the *TV Sutras,* I attuned myself to messages that are broadcast into the living room of my San Francisco apartment. My method: I do a half-hour yoga set while watching the DVD *Peaceful Weight Loss through Yoga.* Then I turn off the DVD player and TV, sit cross-legged on the floor, facing the television, and meditate for twenty minutes. I breathe in, wait, breathe out, wait, breathe in, wait ... try to accept whatever arises, internally or externally. I do not close my eyes because closed eyes equal duality, I've been told, while open eyes equal oneness. When my mind wanders, I say to myself "thinking," and refocus on my breath. When I finish meditating, I crawl off my cushion and turn the TV back on. Words and images emerge. There's a flash of recognition and my hand scribbles furiously: I transcribe the first words that strike me, then briefly I describe the scene from which the TV sutra arose. I take a breath, scoot against the wall and quickly write my commentary. Sometimes my interpretation surprises me. Sometimes I disagree with it. But I write down whatever comes. I do not attempt irony, cleverness or perfection—or art. The *TV Sutras* are totally in-the-moment sincere, even if that sincerity makes me cringe afterwards. The 78 sutras were received between July 14 and December 2, 2009.

It's good to see you.

Petite woman talking to dark-haired man.

COMMENTARY

Now the teachings begin. Showing up is the first step.

2

FDA approved.

Voiceover. Image of woman with big dark eyes.

COMMENTARY

This is the right path to be taking.

3

Do you believe I'm in more deep shit than you are.

Dark haired man talking to blonde woman in car.

COMMENTARY

Do not be discouraged by past difficulties. It's all a continuum.
Start where you are.

Hey, hey, you scored.

Man and woman frantically looking for child in crowd. Two orange balloons high in sky. Street vendor exclaims, "Hey, hey, you scored!" but woman ignores him.

COMMENTARY

Do not be so caught up in frantic seeking and grasping that you can't acknowledge the blessings in front of you. Grace appears in the most unlikely of circumstances.

Do you want me to come back to your place?

Man and woman in bar.

COMMENTARY

Focus on getting back to the basics/beginning anew. Establish a home base you can return to.

6

[Silent sutra.]

Woman at desk writing. She finishes a manuscript, a novel, smiling proudly. She ties it with a piece of twine and inserts a red rose in the twine.

COMMENTARY

The grace of a project well done. No words are necessary when you're in a state of perfect harmony. At some point, the breath you breathe will be your final breath. Take in the glory of each breath, its preciousness.

7

I haven't done those kind of movies in years.

Woman bartender talking to man. She's smiling. Man is discombobulated because she's misunderstanding his offer. As the woman looks back fondly, she's sexy, with a twinkle in her eye.

COMMENTARY

Time to own the past, to allow that energy to infuse the present. Allow desire back into your life, the freshness of encounter.

Stops more leaks than the next leading brand.

End of tampon commercial.

COMMENTARY

Think of all the friends you've fallen out with. This is a sort of leaking, the leaking away of love. Distraction and lack of focus are also forms of leaking: losing track of what is valuable and meaningful. Practice is a form of containment, a means to hold what is most dear.

I don't understand why we should part at prom when it's our last prom. We should have a good time.

Young woman with long straight hair talking to unseen interviewer.

COMMENTARY

Take pleasure in existence. Savor the connections between self and others, between self and body. Savor each moment in this festival of evanescence.

Think what you like, but I want to get in that room and inter-rogate him myself.

Woman in suit talking with man in suit.

COMMENTARY

We must experience things for ourselves rather than relying on the word of others. We must be forceful and vigorous in pursuing our path, in seeking entry into new worlds.

Right in this dressing room, look at it.

Voiceover by man remembering being a baby in a soccer locker room. Pix of locker room with baby superimposed.

COMMENTARY

Look at what is before you. When you *really* look at it, the present always resonates back to your origins. Look at the world with the freshness of an infant. Focus not on the game itself, but on the sanctuary of preparation, your practice/personal sanctuary. Be present in it.

in be—be in—be g in—begin

Flat blue background, bold white sans serif "in" appears, then beside it, "be." They switch places, then a "g" joins them and they fuse together to form "begin." Simultaneously, the words are sung by a chorus of unseen Muppets. A book floats across the screen and opens.

COMMENTARY

Now is the time to begin, to be in. Rest inward, be grounded within yourself, and the book will get written. Think of a new project as a pleasurable, light experience rather than a burden or task. Take joy in writing.

A is for Arthur, B is for bear, C is for computer. At the library, at the library, get yourself a card and you've got yourself a key.

ABCs sung by unseen woman. Images flash to represent the words. Library refrain sung by unseen chorus.

COMMENTARY

Proceed with openness; the answers are waiting for you. Arthur = the realm of myth/the primordial. Bear = animal nature. Connect to these forces and sit down to the computer, write— find the key.

14

Wait for me, driver. I'll be right back.

Man getting out of cab.

COMMENTARY

Keep returning to the practice. It will always be there waiting
for you. Life will also be waiting for you—no need to cling to
it during practice. This is the key to focus. Leave competing
demands behind.

"Betsy!" "Okay, Dad." "Joan!" "Okay, Dad."

Man asleep. Woman asleep. Alarm ringing. Both try to shut it off. Man succeeds. Puts feet in slippers. Closes window. Goes to closet, gets robes for himself and wife. The two exchange meaningful eye contact. Man goes down hall, knocks on door, and shouts "Betsy!" Girl shouts back, "Okay, Dad." Then man shouts, "Joan," and girl shouts back, "Okay, Dad." Man takes cover off bird cage. Bird tweets.

COMMENTARY

When it's time to awaken, get up, heed the call. Proceed in a calm, centered manner, purposely taking one step after the other. Make an intention and follow through. Help others with their intents as well. Focus on action rather than analysis. Create purposeful rituals and follow them.

Who says you have to have 12 periods a year on the pill.

Montage of young women repeating, "Who says."

COMMENTARY

Each of us progresses, unfolds at our own speed. There is no set route. Acknowledge and follow your own rhythm. Trust your own experience/authority over societal expectations/programmatic doctrine.

You ready? One. Two. Three.

Two men lift top off of something.

COMMENTARY

Be prepared. Take your time. Counting breaths will lead you to accomplishing your goals. Seek support when you need it. Rest in the preparation, focus on the present, and the future will gracefully unfold.

"How's Roger?" "Roger's the most boring person I know."

Woman working at the computer. Another woman enters. Woman at computer says, "How's Roger." Other woman answers, "Roger's the most boring person I know." Woman continues typing.

COMMENTARY

When focusing, don't resist outside thoughts or distractions. Welcome them, let them have their say, and then continue with focus. You'll never get rid of distractions. The point is to return.

19

Here we are. I haven't thrown anything away.

Slowly dancing sock monkey. Cut to two men entering a room stuffed with file boxes and papers. Older man with bushy hair speaks to younger man.

COMMENTARY

Rest in the present, fully embodying the moment. To be focused doesn't mean you have to get rid of anything, get rid of your complexity. Rather, it allows you to fully own all parts of yourself. When you close the door in order to practice, you can always open the door afterwards, and all your stuff will be waiting for you, just like you left it.

20

[Silent sutra.]

Car blocking busy intersection. Man angrily honking horn. A group of men pushes car to get it moving. Car goes over the hill, rolls away. Driver frantically chases car, jumps in and takes over wheel. Long crazy ride as car slowly loses steam. Man turns the car and it coasts to a stop, only to land on a street elevator, which raises car in the air. Driver motions to boy to switch elevator to down. Boy does, and car drives away.

COMMENTARY

When you move energy/sit down to practice, the energy/mind can run out of control. Jump in the driver's seat, take charge of the wheel, ride the energy/thoughts until they coast out of steam. When new challenges arise, confront them and they will become manageable. Proceed with a balance of passive and active approaches—and don't hesitate to ask for assistance.

21

"Are you coming in?" "Stay just as you are or you'll never finish that book."

Man opens a square manhole, crawls down into a tunnel, opens another door, takes out gun, walks into room. Man sitting at desk says, "You coming in?" Man points gun and says, "Stay just as you are or you'll never finish that book."

COMMENTARY

When distractions enter, you must maintain your focus, not panic before them. They'll go to great lengths to find you, burrowing up from the depths of your unconscious. You can't keep them out, can't attain a life without distractions. What matters is not being thrown off course when they arise. Do not be shaken by the assault. Stay as you are. Finish your book.

"The medulla oblongata is where anger, jealousy, and aggression come from. And where does happiness come from? What does Mama say?" "Momma says happiness comes from the rays of sunshine beaming down from the blue sky."

College classroom. Professor who looks like Colonel Sanders is lecturing. He asks happiness question. Male student stands and answers.

COMMENTARY

Do not be fatalistic when confronting your body/genetic heritage. Genetics is but a blueprint. No need to look for happiness—it's all around you, beaming down. Open yourself to receive it.

Just a few weeks ago we were sitting in Orlando—and now we're being flown to Las Vegas for the most amazing dream that anyone could have.

Man and smiling woman sitting in car, man with arm around woman, man speaking.

COMMENTARY

Be ready for the unexpected. Life is change. Amazing shifts are possible if you keep yourself open to them.

Today Laura decided to show that bladder who's boss.

Smiling, proud woman walking.

COMMENTARY

We all have our physical limitations. Rather than feeling victimized by your body, take an active role in your healing. Create a dialogue with the body, transcend the mind/body split.

Put good in, put good out.

Orange juice commercial.

COMMENTARY

Be aware of your influences, of what you take in. We consume on all levels of our being. Be conscious in your choices. Life is a process of exchange. We are never alone in this, but a beat in a much larger pattern. Inhalation/exhalation. Stay with the breath. We are a conduit of exits as well as entrances.

26

His enthusiasm just carried over.

Man speaking. In comfortable suit and mock turtleneck against a pale gray background that gradates to dark gray at the bottom of the screen. He must be sitting on a stool.

COMMENTARY

Be committed and excited about your practice. Rather than viewing it as work, approach it with pleasure. Then all background distractions will fade and you will feel the joy of this moment, this engagement.

27

We can't ask to be your friends if we rob you and humiliate you.

Military officers talking around a conference table.

COMMENTARY

Be kind to yourself, have patience—behave in a manner that allows you to trust yourself. Gain your own trust through kindness, gentleness, responsibility. Befriend yourself, take care of yourself.

There's also a section for your favorite TV shows, movies, documentaries. All your favorite genres.

Man sitting on stool, blue background, holding a printed guide.

COMMENTARY

Practice does not mean turning your back on life. Through practice you can fully immerse yourself in life, embrace its variety, its array of excitements.

29

What happened to "mine is yours," baby? We're married now.

Man and woman fighting over giant check, woman speaking.

COMMENTARY

Stop struggling over materialism/duality. Accept that the mind and body are one. Consumerism rules when you get lost in your separateness. Focus on your oneness within the material realm. Let go of the struggle, and materialism will no longer dominate you.

30

You're looking at that moss like it's going to sing to you.

Standing man talking to man crouched on ground in nature setting.

COMMENTARY

Rejoice in your surroundings—open yourself, listen. The simplest things are glorious—no need to search—look at what's right in front of you. Teachers are everywhere.

A woman to adore you, to take care of you.

Woman caressing a man's head adoringly and talking.

COMMENTARY

Treat yourself with the tenderness and affection of a lover. It is a joy to take care of yourself, to honor your presence in the world, your uniqueness. When you are filled with desire, you are eager to keep your promises.

Maybe they're right—maybe there is more to life than meets the eyes. What the hell do I know.

Two men and a woman entering a room, woman talking.

COMMENTARY

Look beyond the surface of things. Be humble in your knowledge of the world, open to new, unsuspected layers unfurling.

"You really had a very narrow escape, you know." "I know."

Man and woman drinking cocktails. Man speaks, woman answers.

COMMENTARY

Remember the calm after the storm. When we're in the midst of trauma, it feels like that's all there is—but no matter how treacherous our situation, things can shift. Celebrate all the ways you have survived thus far—the misfortunes that lead you to seek calm.

34

Please don't turn me into them, into anybody.

Young boy talking to middle-aged woman, who tells him he's safe at her home.

COMMENTARY

Practice will not turn you into a drone. It is a safe place; relax into it. It will make you more of yourself, not less. Taking responsibility does not mean turning your back on your playfulness, your childlike qualities—it's giving those qualities a safe haven.

Piggy banks were not harmed in the planning of this party.

Colorful animation of playful piggy banks, voiceover.

COMMENTARY

Take a playful attitude towards your practice. In a committed practice, your playful side need not be harmed. Do not think of practice as work. Take pleasure in it. Play.

36

With a graffiti-strewn backdrop, this field hardly looks like a field of dreams.

Voiceover. Images of baseball field.

COMMENTARY

Look beyond the surface—what at first seems unpromising may unfold surprising potential, excitement. Remove your self-limiting blinders.

[Silent sutra.]

Huge rainstorm/floods, huge flocks of birds crashing through huge glass walls and domed ceilings. Young boy dives into torrential water, swims beneath and captures a clear jewel in the palm of his hand. Amid all the chaos, this is the sole point of his focus. He has captured the miraculous.

COMMENTARY

This is practice personified, the calm we can find beneath the torrents of the mind.

I warned him.

Said by man loading gun. Cut to another man lying on the floor in a pool of blood.

COMMENTARY

Own your actions/decisions. Don't apologize. Move on. Pay heed to warning signs, and change your course accordingly. You *can* change the outcome.

39

A perfect man. Never in politics his whole life.

Men in room discussing appointment of young man to Senate.

COMMENTARY

Approach the world with freshness, as if you were seeing it for the first time. Surprising insights can come from the position of naiveté.

All the princes are nothing, nothing.

Bearded old man in raggedy robe stumbling around some stone ruins, ranting, his words echoing.

COMMENTARY

Do not look for authority outside yourself, do not buy into cultural hierarchies. Focus on the echo—one's words, one's self are not separated from the rest of the world. One speaks, and the world answers back.

"These busts look like a mausoleum. Bad for the patients, don't you think?" "I think the busts are rather handsome."

Man in military officer's uniform sitting in chair. Looks quizzically up at a statue on a ledge above and behind him, then looks guiltily at nun/nurse sitting at desk facing him. Man speaks, nun/nurse replies.

COMMENTARY

Nothing has just one meaning. Many different views can be brought to any situation. Do not be afraid to look at mortality—one can find beauty there, healing potentials. With a shift in perspective, death need not be scary. At the very least, do not resist its existence.

I read somewhere that girls my age become quiet within themselves and begin to think about the miracle that's taking place within their bodies.

Voiceover. Image of young girl sitting in front of window, leaning on table, chin resting on clasped hands, looking contemplative.

COMMENTARY

Practice is not about denying the body. It's about tuning in to it, the mind and body resonating. The body is ever-changing— welcome, take pleasure in those changes, for they are truly miraculous. Pay attention to texts you come across, for they can point the way within.

Don't worry, it's good to get some blood flowing into my head.

Boy dragging man through woods on a stretcher made of branches. Boy attempts to pull man across two logs stretched across shallow crossing in river. Man capsizes, lands in river, speaks.

COMMENTARY

Look beyond preconceptions, and make the most of any given situation. Even a disaster could have useful consequences. Stay present for all the nuances of an event.

At the end of the semester, I feel so tired and want a clean slate.

Girl sitting in classroom, looking forlorn. Voiceover cuts to her speaking, wiping away tears.

COMMENTARY

Do not hold on to the energy of the past. Each day is an opportunity to begin again. Nothing is pure. When you face distractions, return to your intent.

You can identify reliable companies just by looking. Start with trust.

Voiceover. Images of website and list of company names. White type on blue background.

COMMENTARY

Approach experience with freshness. Without suspicion, pay close attention. Open your heart, and the world will open to you.

46

Find everything you want with name brand products up to 70% off. Every day.

Woman opens a small earring box, and the screen fills with jewels.

COMMENTARY

The treasure chest is not elsewhere, not something you need to strive for. Be present and it will open for you. The slightest things can have enormous potential if you focus your attention on them.

That's probably how we survived it all, we could make each other laugh.

Two women in empty house, looking back on their childhood.

COMMENTARY

Humor is our great salvation. Seek the nuances of a situation, the fissures where awareness is effervescent, flips. It is the beginning of forgiveness.

I have cancer, and it's terminal, and I need to find my father because it feels like a part of me is missing.

Woman sitting on sofa, talking with a man.

COMMENTARY

All life is terminal. Look back and embrace your origins, the long succession of selves and ancestors. We need all of them. We *are* all of them.

49

My life was taking a dark turn, and I started writing about dancing and stripping, and that's it.

Woman talking to a group of people about how her blog got picked up by a Hollywood producer.

COMMENTARY

By delving fully into your experiences—even the difficult ones—you can unleash enormous creative energy. Transformation comes from looking and owning—not denial.

"If he's in trouble I'd be obliged if I could go after him." "I've known that old man for 30 years." "I love him too."

Two cowboys talking, one standing, one on horseback. Standing cowboy = main speaker.

COMMENTARY

When difficult situations arise, address them head-on rather than relying on others to handle them. Even when you screw up, approach yourself with love. Rather than judging, take action to change the situation.

[Silent sutra.]

Woman in store folding shirts, finds a pair of black gloves in pile, looks surprised, gives gloves to another woman to put away. Woman continues folding shirts.

COMMENTARY

We all need to create order, to make sense out of the world. When confronted with something that disrupts that order, examine it to figure out its proper place in your life. Give it its place, and continue with the task at hand. Don't be shaken by surprises—appreciate them. Focus and flexibility are the keys to equanimity.

Fields and woods became my new place of worship, my cathedral.

Boy sitting in woods, sketching a bird. Voiceover of man speaking.

COMMENTARY

Stay in the present, in the natural world. Observe it closely and art will follow from that, a transformation from the present moment to hand, pen, paper. Regardless of subject matter, art begins with embodiment. Spirituality isn't about transcendence. It's resting in immanence.

You're a landlord, Wade. We just rent from you. It's your responsibility.

Group of men sitting around a table, talking.

COMMENTARY

Life is transitory—seek the eternal part of yourself—turn to that part for guidance. Be humble, but not passive. Responsibility is a fluid give-and-take.

54

Every time I look at your face I still see the girl I married 20 years ago, and I always will.

Man and woman in medical clothes, talking. Woman in nurse's uniform, unbuttoned, revealing white bra.

COMMENTARY

Time is not linear—we carry within ourselves all the moments of our lives, simultaneously. Our childhoods haunts our adulthoods. We don't fundamentally change, we grow new layers. Love your layers.

You can't do that.

Man loads rifle in gun store. Clerk says, "You can't do that."
Man blasts clerk with rifle.

COMMENTARY

Resist limiting projections. Be focused, tune into your true
intentions, and proceed. Clarity of intent will carry you through.

There's nothing particularly original about Mona, not even the way she finally brought herself back together again.

Woman alone in hallway lined with lockers, calmly leaning against wall. Male voiceover.

COMMENTARY

The key to balance is in all of us. We don't have to make it up anew. Tune in, listen—if you pay close attention to what you already have, harmony will be restored.

I've come to lift the stone, to raise your voice.

Underground cavern, lights flashing over rippling water. Man enters, voiceover.

COMMENTARY

Be your own hero—turn within—from within the depths of silence you can uncover your true voice.

Sorry. I loved him. I did.

Woman in prison dress, sitting at table, talking to man.

COMMENTARY

Think of consequences before you act. Motivation does not trump action. Only when motivation and action are in harmony should you proceed.

59

[Silent sutra.]

Man brings over gift basket and champagne to another man. Man A is rambling on about how he was spin-doctoring Man B's suicide attempt. In the midst of Man A's chatter, Man B spots a perfect strawberry in the gift basket, reaches down, picks it up and puts it in his mouth. He chews slowly, savoring it.

COMMENTARY

When you rest in the moment, surprising jewels await you. Don't be shaken by the storms of distraction that surround you. Savor the present.

We'll see each other soon. It's not like we're talking forever.

Man talking to woman.

COMMENTARY

Consciousness is not rigid—thoughts flicker in, thoughts flicker out. The point is to return to the breath, return to center. Trust that return.

61

Twenty-two of those forty wins since turning forty.

Voiceover to image of man playing golf.

COMMENTARY

It is never too late to begin. Persevere—your greatest accomplishments may lie ahead.

I simply ask, "Why are things done this way? What are we afraid of?"

Man giving speech to group, outside on grass.

COMMENTARY

Be brave. Rather than relying on formulas and dogmas, question group and personal values. Act according to what you feel is right, not what's expected or how you've acted in the past. Consciousness is an ongoing project, ever adapting.

"My name is Ken Hutchinson, and I'm a cop." "Where did that come from?"

Headshot of man, voiceover: "My name is Ken Hutchinson, and I'm a cop." Man looks confused and says, "Where did that come from?"

COMMENTARY

Cultural labels and rules aren't your true self. They are but clothing the self puts on for a time. Connect to the self beyond societal roles. It is longing to be seen/heard.

I'd go make a cup of tea if I were you, for this may take a while.

Man speaking directly to the camera. Outside, beautiful countryside. Another man has gone to do something with a car.

COMMENTARY

Don't be impatient. Relax and luxuriate in the process.

Look, a unicorn!

Two men in room. Man A yells, "Look, a unicorn!" While Man B looks out the window, Man A grabs something and throws it behind his back so Man B can't see it. Man B turns from window and says, "A unicorn?" Man A: "Sorry, I guess it was just a regular horse."

COMMENTARY

Illusions and fantasies threaten to distract you from your path. Stay focused on what's in front of you rather than distractions that beckon from the sidelines.

Sleep is your body's strongest ally.

Soothing female voiceover to woman sleeping in luxurious ocean blue sheets.

COMMENTARY

Remember to take time out, to rest, to recuperate. Unconsciousness is a place of healing. Let go.

Wait for green before driving through tunnel.

Sign above tunnel as man driving car enters tunnel. Green light above sign. Same sign when man exits tunnel. Red light above sign.

COMMENTARY

Don't be hasty. Prepare before you begin a new task or enter a new phase. Pay attention and you'll know when it's best to wait, best to act.

I'm out there dying for you out of worry.

Woman talking to man.

COMMENTARY

When you fall off center, when you wallow in obsession and fear, remember the deleterious effects on both body and spirit. This is why we practice—to let go of the frenzy, to move from "out there" to the present. To be more fully alive.

We can't do it in silence, you guys. We're going to have to speak to one another.

Woman speaking to small group of people.

COMMENTARY

You aren't just one self, but a community of selves. Welcome the voices within you. Listen.

70

"Is that my costume?" "Yes, I'm sorry. I didn't have anything else to dress up in."

Two women talking at Halloween party. Woman who owns costume is upset.

COMMENTARY

Do not be attached to the roles you take on in life. You do not own those roles. Focus on the self behind those roles. That, no one can co-opt.

Proof—apparitions, hard-core voice phenomena—and we're going to get it.

Men in van driving to a prison. Man speaking.

COMMENTARY

Belief isn't an abstraction—it comes from a close examination of the world you inhabit. You can never prove that your ghosts exist. You can only experience them.

[Silent sutra.]

Woman in bathing suit at poolside. She sits back in a lounge chair, shakes her hair out with her hands, smiles, lies back in chair, and basks in the sun.

COMMENTARY

Luxuriate in the moment, the full is-ness of the present, as if there were no other moment. Pleasure is there for you, if you open yourself to it.

I loved making all those films, even the bad ones.

Man talking to camera.

COMMENTARY

Accept and value all you produce, all aspects of your being. Don't categorize experience as worthy or unworthy. Nothing is a waste.

What was I doing up there anyway, making a speech, me?

Two men sitting in boxcar. Boxcar takes off. Speaker plays harmonica. Big, cloud-studded sky outside door.

COMMENTARY

Accept doubts—they are part of the process, part of being human. Let go of nagging hindsights. Relax, take pleasure in the gloriousness of the present moment.

I have a confession: I'm afraid of horses.

Man talking to woman.

COMMENTARY

Admitting your fears is the first step in dealing with them. Fear is nothing to be ashamed of. Without judgment, look at your fear, name it.

Excuse me sir, this isn't a drinking den. It's a free clinic.

Group of visitors. Visitor man speaking to man in charge.

COMMENTARY

Stay focused on your purpose. Banish elitism from your practice. Practice is as humble as your breath, available to all.

That way isn't as visually appealing, but at least you know if they cheated you out of raisins.

Woman talking to another woman.

COMMENTARY

Look beyond the surface appearance of things; peer *into* the nature of an experience. That's where its value lies—beyond aesthetics, in the nitty-gritty.

It's personal management. The key word is "personal."

Man and woman walking in park, man talking.

COMMENTARY

Structures are helpful, but in the end you need to carve out your own path.

CULTURED

A god grew there, a god grew there,
A wet and weblike god grew there.

—Jack Spicer
(Orpheus after Eurydice)

THE APARTMENT IS A MESS, papers, books and art stacked everywhere, and people who want to be nice compare the squalor to Iris Murdoch's ramshackle bohemian lifestyle. To make room for my forest green rubber yoga mat, I spend several minutes clearing the living room floor. By the door there's a litter box that needs scooping, but I decide I can live with that. While I'm in fish pose, Quincey shits on the floor. I pause the DVD, get paper towels, spray cleaner, odor remover; wipe up the shit, restart the DVD; lie on my back and twist my head upside-down, cat stench still wafting through the tranquil air. Ten minutes later I finish the set, sit cross-legged on my tan crescent-shaped zafu and meditate for twenty minutes; then I turn the TV back on and click the remote three times to switch from DVD to cable mode. An image bursts forth. I copy down the first line of speech that calls to me—usually it's the first thing I hear, but sometimes the words are garbled, sometimes I can tell that the core line of a scene hasn't yet arrived, and I wait. Occasionally the scene just isn't right, so I push the FAV button on the remote until I land on better material. No matter which variation I use, there's always a moment where I feel hailed, hailed by what the TV is saying, and I can proceed with absolute certainty that this is the line for the day. I copy the line, write a brief description of its scene, then I scoot my zafu against the wall (really an overstuffed bookcase) and wait to receive my commentary—I have a moment of doubt, like what could I possibly say about this—but an interpretation is promptly upon me. Books poking into my back, knees up in air, journal and fountain pen in hands, I dash off the sutra's "lesson." I hunt out Kevin, interrupt whatever he's doing on the computer, and read him the day's sutra. "So," he says, "is this project about the banality of the New Age?" Which makes me wonder how seriously I should take my sutras as religious revelation—are they as valid, for instance, as the Ten Commandments? As Joseph Smith with his head in his hat receiving the *Book of Mormon* line by line? Who owns meaning? Only communally sanctioned authority figures? Only scraggly sackcloth-clad prophets starving in forests? Only scraggly loin-clothed prophets starving in caves? Can meaning arise in a depressed middle-aged writer sitting on her living room floor, wearing knit pajama bottoms patterned with hot pink peonies? Where does this meaning come from? Inspired texts, no matter how radical, reflect dominant cultural motifs. William Blake's visions— naked angels, naked chained beings so taut and clenched they look as if they're about to pop a blood vessel, patriarchs with long white beards—are saturated with Christian dogma. Muslims have Muslim visions; Eskimos have Eskimo visions; when I was in a cult we closed our eyes and experienced the inner worlds just as they were written in our sacred texts. In Jack Spicer's metaphor for dictated poetry— that Martians rearrange the furniture in the room—Martians do not add new furniture to the psyche of the poet, they merely rearrange what's already there. When I open myself to receiving my sutra commentary, what is the furniture in my room, what are the texts, classes, conversations, relationships, media bombardments that animate my channeling?

After writing the above I head over to Simply Unique Nails for an emergency pedicure. In an email sent from his meditation retreat, my

Buddhist Teacher lover fantasized giving me a foot massage. I looked down at my mangled toenails, cringed, and Yelped "nail salons in the Castro." As a Vietnamese woman rubs my calluses with scented scrub, I wonder, "Is Kevin right? Is the New Age always banal?" I take a sip of bubbly water, sink into the vibrating lounge chair, and zone out on the flat screen TV. It's *Oprah,* an episode about the daring escapes of child brides held captive by cult leader Tony Alamo. Oprah's camera pans across the outside of the cult's compound, a boxy ranch house in a suburban neighborhood, surrounded by other boxy ranch houses. It looks like the neighborhood I grew up in, except the homes are larger. I flash back to my days in a cult. On the wall beside my bed I thumb-tacked a drawing of a cityscape on Jupiter, radiant with amethyst-spired temples and domes of cobalt and gold, and if I closed my eyes and raised my vibrations, I could leave the tract houses of my youth and visit this realm, where there was so much space between molecules reality itself was effervescent. For an entire decade I was gone. Behind the compound's locked doors and curtained windows, Alamo fucked and humiliated adolescent girls, a harem of more than a dozen "spiritual wives" he beat for the slightest infraction. "When Tony would say that God spoke to him, everyone believed it," says Jeanne, who was 15 when the then 59-year-old Alamo took her as a bride. He took Amy when she was 14, and Desiree when she was 8. I was 25 when I slept with my first spiritual teacher; he had a dark bushy unibrow. The pedicurist holds up a bottle of vermillion polish. "This one?" I nod and imagine my Buddhist Teacher lover putting my shiny toes in his mouth. Jeanne says she cried so hard she broke blood vessels, she says that even though she doesn't believe in suicide, she prayed for God to take her in her sleep. In his email my Buddhist Teacher lover said at 5:30 in the morning he was sitting in the meditation hall, surrounded by 200 students, all of them silently observing their breaths; he thought of me and was hit by "full blown arousal." Thinking of this turns me on, and I squirm in my massage chair. The pedicurist barks, "Please be still. These clippers very sharp." My Buddhist Teacher lover said our past life connections fueled his erection, and even though I know better, I wrote back, yes, yes, our love reaches back through time, misty white trails of previous incarnations curl about us like hookah smoke. As I type this I can feel Kevin sitting at his desk, rolling his eyes and groaning, "Banal." "But it feels so—significant," I argue. Behind all those rainbows, unicorns, feel-good slogans, deprivations and rituals, behind the closed doors of the temple, there's a meaning machine in libidinal overdrive. Perhaps it's not the trappings but meaning itself that's banal. *Banal* comes from *ban,* a widely disseminated proclamation, which comes from the Indo-European *bha,* to speak. The French *boulin à ban* or *four à ban* was a mill or an oven shared by the tenants of a feudal lord. In both English and French, banal came from this idea of the commons. Isn't that the promise—or at least the hope—of the *TV Sutras,* that meaning is a sort of commons, available to everyone? Bride Nikki staged a daring escape, but when she made her way home, her mother shunned her, at Alamo's behest. I leave a $10 tip and walk into a drizzly October evening. When I turn the key in the ignition, rain splashes down in torrents, as if a twist of my wrist switched on the weather. My Toyota floats over the glistening asphalt—umbrellaed pedestrians appear before the windshield in flashes, stark and lurid as zombies. My faceted rose quartz bracelet sparkles in the streetlight. On the CD player Antony and the Johnsons croon, over and over, "It's such a mystery to me."

If Kevin were doing the *TV Sutras* he'd include the names of the movies or TV shows, and the stars who are speaking. He'd reveal that Chevy Chase spoke Sutra 73, Woody Allen spoke Sutra 78, silent Sutra 6 is mimed by Winona Ryder, Cary Grant is the dad in Sutra 15, Farrah Fawcett wears the prison dress in Sutra 58, the obnoxious wife in Sutra 29 is Cameron Diaz, Rock Hudson is the disillusioned soldier in Sutra 41. Most of the details I've forgotten. In Sutra 22 when Adam Sandler says, "Momma says happiness comes from the rays of sunshine beaming down from the blue sky," there's no mention of where the sunshine's beaming down, if Momma observed the sunshine at home, in a field, on a vacation in Hawaii; the precise blue of the sky, the temperature, the breeze; how Sandler or Momma measure or define happiness; where Momma was when she said this, what she was doing, how often she has said it, etc. The generality of slogans provides a screen onto which we can project our own lives. Slogans are generous that way. Momma is right here, sitting beside me in bed as I type this; she's jolly and smells of garlic, and even though it's a drizzly day, sunlight is streaming in through my window. Momma is sitting beside you too, in your bed or on the couch, or a bus, or in a molded plastic chair in McDonalds, or a musty college library—wherever it is you're reading this, Momma is sitting right there with you. Do you feel her love, or is she giving you that *get your ass together* glare? Naming creates comfort, distance. Winona Ryder up on the screen = not me. Out from the generality of sutras, stick figures point back at us, their bony fingers jabbing YOU—YOU—YOU! So that's why I don't name names.

When his wife, Susan, dies of cancer, Alamo dresses her embalmed body in a wedding gown—for she is the bride of God—and puts her on display in his dining room. He announces to the world that he and Susan are immortal prophets—and that Susan will rise from the dead. Local DJs play "Wake Up, Little Susie" and laugh. He commands his students to stand around her casket and pray for her resurrection, which they do, in two-hour shifts, twenty-four hours a day, for eighteen months. Day after day twelve-year-old Elishah lies down beside the rotting body. Susan is cold and really, really hard. She smells. Each day the corpse does not open its eyes, Elishah and other children are beaten by senior students. The senior students use two-by-six boards drilled with holes. Sometimes Alamo grabs Elishah's face, strokes it, then spits in it. He says the devil is in the children. At the compound's cafeteria, students eat spoiled food gathered from grocery stores and garbage bins. In the cult's school, students learn that the Pope had JFK assassinated and dinosaurs didn't exist. Alamo finally entombs Susan's body in a heart-shaped mausoleum and declares she will return to him in the body of a younger woman.

Sutra literally means a thread or line that holds things together. It is derived from the verbal root siv-, meaning to sew. I think of embroidery, the precise knots and stitches my grandmother taught me to make flowers appear on pillowcases. Sutras were designed for concision, easily memorized by students. From the *Vayu Purana:* "Of minimal syllabary, unambiguous, pithy, comprehensive, non-redundant, and without flaw: who knows the sutras knows it to be thus." Where do sutras come from? They are received by an enlightened/god-crazed being, passed on, and eventually collected. *By self-control on the primal activator comes knowledge of the hidden, the subtle, and the distant.* Patanjali (sometime between 400 B.C. and 200 A.D.), the author of the *Yoga Sutras* , was not just a great sage, but an incarnation of Vishnu. *The very existence of the seen is for the sake of the seer.* Flowers rained down from the heavens when Atisha (980–1054 A.D.), the recipient of the Tibetan Buddhist lojong slogans, was born. A rainbow canopy appeared, and the gods sang hymns which brought gladness and joy to all people. On the eve of his wedding, the goddess Tara appeared to Atisha and warned him against the ephemeral pleasures of marriage. *As an elephant sinks deeply into the swamp, the hero would sink in the mire of lust.* Atisha abandoned his bride and set off on his spiritual quest. To clarify the unrelenting pithiness of the sutras, later practitioners write commentaries, filtered through their own cultural perspectives—but the original words of the enlightened beings are never changed. Kevin doesn't believe this, and he suggests I write extra *TV Sutras* and edit out the weaker ones. "Like Moses," he says. "Maybe God really gave Moses 14 commandments." I say, no, no, no, you can't do that for a conceptual piece. Yet, having been married to me for 26 years, he knows I'm never as pure as I claim to be. In my commentary for Sutra 25—*Put good in, put good out*—I excised the line, "By making

healthy choices we can be a more harmonious being in the world."
It sounded so proscriptive—and stupid—"Healthy Choice" being a
brand of diet TV dinners. Images came flooding in of well-scrubbed,
glowing rosy cheeks, of WASP-y women in comfortable shoes—if I
look in the mirror, this kind of describes me. Over breakfast at a
poetry conference, an academic interrupted my morning chatter and
declared, "You are *so* Midwestern," and this troubled me for years.
Kevin turns back to the computer and begins typing. He's writing
about New Narrative, how it reclaimed what was considered vulgar
in poetry. New Narrative Dodie versus New Age Dodie. Can one
ever stop embarrassing the other? Dare I reclaim what's considered
vulgar in spirituality? Bring on those crazed ascetics rushing from
the forest to the Ganges, slaying any hoi polloi who step in their
path! Bring on crucified Jesus oozing blood and horror. Bring on
those horny gurus who fuck their students into enlightenment.
*Understand your attachments, your aversions, and your indifference,
and love them all.*

Stubby white utility candles stand upright in globs of wax Nance
and I have dripped onto mayonnaise jar lids. Shadows tremble across
the basement's cinder block walls; our eleven-year-old fingers hover
on the tear-drop shaped planchette. It begins to move slowly, in
little circles, then jerks across the Ouija board in violent, purposeful
jags. The spirit spells out, "F-U-C-K-Y-O-U-R-P-U-S-S-Y." The
spirit always talks dirty. Nance and I are lovers, but that's a big
secret—even from each another. The sex happens during our weekly
sleepovers, when she pretends to be unconscious. She talks to me in

her sleep—I name a boy or a Beatle, and her dreaming self channels that boy or Beatle. "You are so luvly, my luv," the voice says in a British accent. Ghostly fingers and mouth roam across my body, sucking and prodding, until I climax. The orgasms astonish and terrify me—like they don't belong to me, like my groin has been possessed by this ravenous elsewhere—a clenching so brutal it could rip a phonebook in two. I can't get enough of them. Ten years later Nance and I, fully awake lovers, will join the cult. The bedroom we share in a house with other cult members has impossibly high ceilings, windows with thick wooden frames stretching from knee-high to heaven; light floods in, flickering through leafy Indiana oaks and elms, the two of us moving in slow motion, writhing on the mattress on the floor, our spirits swelling, filling the room, bouncing against the cracked 19th-century ceiling—we are great chords of being, gliding and spasming, our whirly-wind chakras twirling in unison. Spiritual lesbian sex is much better than our drugged lesbian sex of the past couple of years.

It's 1972. Sandy looks radiant in her long orange Indian smock. She never cared for orange until receiving her third initiation. But ever since then she's felt drawn to it, for the third initiation links you to the Causal Plane, and the color of the Causal Plane is orange. My reaction to this is a big wow. Sandy is confident, beautiful, charismatic. She plans to be a stewardess when she graduates. Single-handedly she brought the cult to Indiana University. Being the senior student, she led our study groups. We sat in living rooms on folding chairs and boxy thrift store couches and read "discourses" together—a thin stack of 8 1/2 x 11 pages with a cover sheet of pale blue paper, stapled in the top left corner. We listened to the music of Cesar Franck because it was spiritual. We tried not to listen to rock music. We didn't do drugs, but we loved to share stories of our former acid trips. We fasted every Friday, which my friends and I would fudge on by declaring that Thursday dinner through Friday dinner was 24 hours. We formed a Break Your Fast Club, and every Friday at 6:00 on the dot we'd meet at the Sizzler and gorge on steak and baked potatoes, then moan about our belly aches. We entered into pyramid marketing schemes, selling one another vitamins and speedy herbal liquids. Sandy's mother, Pat, who lived three hours north, learned from another cultist how to draw portraits with pastels, and she made lots of money driving her van to craft fairs and doing quick sketches of Midwestern tourists. Pat came to Indiana University and gave a workshop on pastel portraiture. Some of my friends were naturals, and they too made money on the fair circuit. Since neither Nance nor I could manage a pastel that looked human, let alone recognizable, we decided to make stuffed animals. We tried to adapt a stuffed dog pattern into a unicorn, but the horn came out lopsided and limp. The musically inclined composed songs about Soul and played them at gatherings on acoustic guitars. We drank ginseng tonic and chanted in the New Year in a one-room red brick schoolhouse in the middle of a field, snow glittering in the moonlight. We hugged and smiled and opened our hearts to one another. Bloomington was a pod of ultimate love and safety, and like the Cottingley fairies frolicking among the harebells, we were so full of high vibes our flesh beat translucent. I embraced the teachings, and my grades went down. For the first time in my life I was sort of popular.

Through Open University, Nance and I gave introductory talks in the student union center, and every Thursday between 7 and 10 p.m. we sat in the lobby of IU's library, handing out "literature." One evening my French conversation teacher stopped by our table. "Bonsoir, Mademoiselle Bellamy." He was a grad student, probably not much older than I, but his sophistication put him in an untouchable age bracket. My French conversational skills were atrocious, rarely moving beyond infinitives—I to go to the market, I to drink le café au lait—but I was his favorite, being the only student in the class interested in French literature. Our longing to share our passion for French literature remained unfulfilled, for I wasn't allowed to speak English and who could discuss anything with my crippled French. He was a stickler for speaking French. Once a week our class would meet in the French Department lounge for French Coffee Hour—any Frenchophile could drop by and sip strong coffee while conversing in French. The third week my cute teacher caught a group of us goofing around in English, and he went ballistic. "How dare you speak English during French Coffee Hour!" he shouted in French. Then he revoked our French Coffee Hour privileges. Now that I teach, I realize this hurt him more than it did us, as it gave him an extra class a week to prep for and lead. "Pas du French Coffee Hour!" my friends and I roared after class. Because of my enthusiasm for Sartre and Racine, he eventually forgave my transgressions and mercifully gave me a B. I to thank you for such a bonne grade. And suddenly here he is in front of the folding table Nance and I have set up in the library lobby with its brown-speckled floor reflecting banks of florescent overheads, his dark hair and intense eyes witnessing my life outside of class, seeing me as a spiritual person competent at answering *his* questions for a change. "I've come to see the moon rocks," he said in glorious English. This was a couple of years after the Apollo moonwalk, and across the lobby was a vitrine displaying some rocks they'd brought back, a vial full of gravel. "The moon rocks are crummy," I said. "You don't need to go to the moon to experience other worlds," I added with a flourish and handed him a pamphlet. "In actuality, we all have five bodies," I told him, "and three of them are located in our head." "Le tête," I added, pointing to my temple. "*La* tête," he laughed and walked on. In truth, I was frightened of those moon rocks. In 1968—a year before the moonwalk—the first Western Master predicted that a moon virus was going to wipe out most of humanity, and civilization as we knew it would end in 1975. What if the moon virus was in that vial, powerful enough to leak through safety glass, waft through the moist summer air, and cling to the fine hairs in my nostrils, and in just a few years the teeming library lobby would be empty, the Souls of students and professors alike having translated to other planes— in cult lingo "to translate" is "to die"—the overhead fluorescents would have died out too, and all would be silence and darkness, save for a faint scratching of cockroach feet. When 1975 came and went, and civilization seemed just fine, some cultists said the plague had happened on another plane. Others later suggested the moon virus was the Master's metaphor for AIDS.

1974. Nance and I have graduated and are both working in a dorm cafeteria—the only job we could find in Bloomington. Our supervisor, a strict Christian lady, granted us a week off to attend a "religious" meeting, and thus we made our way to the cult's yearly national convention, in Jacksonville, Florida. This is the first time I've flown on a plane, stayed in a hotel, left the Midwest, seen a palm tree or the living Master. The living Master has both an inner and an outer form. The inner Master is perfect, all-knowing, and with each of us at all times. The outer Master is human and we're not supposed to worship him. After registration, I sit in the lush hotel lobby, fiddling with my nametag. Beneath my name and "Bloomington, IN" is printed the cult's symbol, a royal blue and marigold bulls-eye. Nance ran up to the room to get her camera, and she's taking forever. The black leather armchair is so plush, I could sink into it and disappear. I stare vacantly at a giant potted bromeliad. The leaves—if you'd call them that, the green part—remind me of a banana peel, when the peel is still attached to the banana, in sections, arching backwards—a series of waxy green banana peels stacked one inside the other, and from the center pokes a trumpet of magenta, too intensely magenta for this world, its "petals" sharply pointed—like razors—the incandescent dentata of an alien vagina. To live among such plants I would have to be someone else—the kind of person who wears a floor-length dashiki—purple velvet, with intricate metallic trim—and has kohl-lined eyes. I'd smell of frankincense and Salems, which I'd wave in a foot-long cigarette holder as I call everybody "dahling." I'd walk with a slight limp and take on younger lovers who I'd parade through expensive seafood restaurants where I always pick up the check as white-aproned waiters raise their eyebrows. Hidden speakers broadcast a muted instrumental of "My Funny Valentine." A woman's voice says, "I wonder what sign the Master is." It's from a young woman on the black leather sofa directly across from me. There's a bromeliad beside her too. She has on sandals and a long blue floral skirt. Braless nipples indent her pale yellow tank top, as if the very thought of the Master's sign excites her. She adds quickly, "I don't want to know, I don't want to limit him like that." Her friend, who's dressed almost exactly the same, chimes in, "The Master is of all signs." They yes-shake their heads up and down, flipping their long center-parted hair in unison. These two have more flair than the cultists I know in Bloomington—except for Sandy. They remind me of the hippie girls who leap for Frisbees in the meadow in front of the student union building, perfectly lean in cut-offs so short white flaps of pocket dangle from leg holes, girls radiant with heterosexuality, with tanned toothy boyfriends who take them hiking in Central America. Our cult wasn't against queerness per se—Nance and I felt fully accepted in the community. We didn't know any other lesbian cultists, but we were friends with a number of gay men. One of them was Troy, who took Nance and me to our first drag bar, in Indianapolis. I've written about this before but omitted the cult connection—because I rationalized it was superfluous to the experience, because I didn't want anybody to know how deeply a fool was I. For ten years this was my life, for ten years I was gone. It was at the home of a gay cultist in Indianapolis that I saw my first ginger jar lamp. Five years later when I moved to San Francisco, I purchased a ginger jar lamp for my sparse studio apartment, still longing to be as sophisticated as that aging Midwestern queen. Queer cultists kept things from getting too goody-goody. Homosexuality is Soul's karmic choice, we were taught in books and lectures. Homosexuality is a learning experience, neither good nor bad. Like cigarettes and alcohol, as a student progresses spiritually, same-sex desire will drop away. If Nance and I were appalled by this attitude, we didn't talk about it. We didn't talk about a lot of things. As graduation approached, our relationship was feeling like a time bomb, tick tick ticking, and the promise of future, more spiritual, queer-free selves didn't help. The blue-skirted cultist on the left says, "I'm a Virgo," and the blue-skirted cultist on the right replies, "I thought so!" And then the first blue-skirted woman says, "I wonder if the Master is a Virgo like me." I consider chiming in, "Sandy told me the Master is a Capricorn, and her mother's a higher initiate, so she would know," but it seems wrong to interrupt their happy indeterminacy. They'd probably consider me coarse, delivering a fact about the Master that's so mundane he's transcended it. The Master is of all signs—it makes perfect sense. Capricorn is a goat, but the Master soars like an eagle.

Nance finally arrives, waving her camera at me—"Found it!"—and we head over to the Golden Tao, a vegetarian restaurant recommended in our registration packet. At the top of the list are also a couple of veggie-friendly Chinese restaurants. The cult values vegetables. Sandy said that if we found ourselves in a situation where a fast-food cheeseburger was the only option, we should ask for extra tomato and lettuce to amp up the nutrition. There's lots of time until the evening session, so Nance and I languorously stroll along the St. Johns River, which is vast, more like a lake than a river. We're impressed. "Wow, it's so wide!" Nance snaps a few pictures. She drops the camera in her patchwork leather shoulder bag and pulls out a Downtown Jacksonville brochure. "It says here that Harriet Beecher Stowe used to live along the river." "*Uncle Tom's Cabin!*" I exclaim. Sandy told us the book was dictated to Stowe by spirit authors. Nance makes her eyes go wide and holds her arms out in front of her like she's sleepwalking and speaks in a deep monotone: "Harriet, are you ready? Okay, write: 'I'm—your—cult—now!'" I laugh, even though she's done this before. I say, "Did they have slaves in Florida?" Nance shrugs and continues reading. "It says, quote unquote, 'The St. Johns has a very slow flow rate at a third of a mile an hour, and is often described as lazy.' That's funny, a lazy river. It says that sometimes you can spot dolphins and sharks!" We look, our heads swiveling left then right. The surface is a placid sheen. No fish at all. "What about the water," I say, "the salt—rivers don't have salt, right? So how can ocean animals move from salt to no salt?" The air smells not of sea, but of coffee, with an undernote of lemon. Nance says, "Listen to this. 'It is one of a small number of rivers in the United States to run north.'" We grin at each other. "How perfect," I say, "a river that runs the wrong way." To prepare us for the trip, Sandy explained that the presence of the Master alters the ecology of the lower worlds, that wherever he appears the weather goes crazy. "With the Master in town, I'm surprised the river doesn't run sideways!" jokes Nance. I laugh. Sandy said that the week before last year's convention in Anaheim, there were wildfires. And this year it was rain, major thunderstorms that practically shut down the city. The concierge told us he's never seen storms like this, not in Jacksonville in November. Whenever there's a large gathering of cultists, Spirit arrives ahead of time to raise the vibrations of the area. This threatens the negative forces and they attack Spirit, and their clash manifests in violent weather. The storms suddenly stopped last night, when all the students were arriving. Everybody was talking about it at registration. People said that our gathering together generated an immense amount of light and sound, enough to overpower the negative forces. It's really exciting. I say to Nance, "I don't think the river is lazy; it's magnificently calm, not all that churning like Lake Michigan. This would be a wonderful place for a Master to be born." A Master is always born under strange circumstances near a large body of water. "Why water," I say. "What do you think it does?" Nance tenses her lips and looks up at nothing in particular, like she's thinking really hard. She pushes her wire rims up her nose and says, "Maybe it captures the negative energies so the Master can enter this plane safely, you know, like how you're not supposed to take a bath during a storm because you'll get electrocuted, like the water attracts the lightning. Can you imagine how crazy the weather must be when a Master is born!" She shakes her head from side to side and shouts, "Wowie zowie!" I love it when she's enthused; she's sexy, the curve of her jawbone when she pushes her brown bob behind her ears—and those little oval wire rims that make her look so smart, like John Lennon. I wish I wanted her more. She deserves to be wanted more.

The Golden Tao is packed with cultists—you can pick us out by our nametags, our kindness, our scrubbed joviality. The wait staff loves us and we love the wait staff, for the wait staff like us are Souls working off karma. Our tempeh Reubens were so delicious we decided to split a hot carob fudge goat milk ice cream sundae. Just as Nance and I dip into the melty goo, we hear whispers all around us, excited whispers. "Over there." "It's her." "It's Neva Novak." "It's Neva, from the planet Jupiter." "Where?" "By the door." A platinum blonde woman whooshes into the restaurant. She has high cheekbones and an upturned nose. A sheer dress floats about her petite body, layer upon irregular layer of pale blue chiffon, perforated throughout with large holes. Another whisper: "Clothing on Jupiter has holes because reality is more permeable there." Noticing all the stares, Neva raises her arms above her head and twirls, her diaphanous dress fluttering after her. She stops beside the gold-plated tortoise fountain and bows. Nance and I applaud. The whole room applauds. Nance says, "Wowie zowie—Neva Novak!" I take a bite of sundae, smile goofily and shake my shoulders like I'm quivering with joy. Hot carob drips down my chin. Neva is a walk-in from Ganymede, the largest moon of Jupiter. The people of Jupiter, the Jovians, exist at a higher level of vibration, on the Astral Plane. Neva lived for 212 Jupiter years on the Astral Plane, until she was instructed by her leaders to bring to Earth a message of peace and brotherhood. In 1955 she took over the life of a seven-year-old girl who died in a bus wreck in Tennessee. Eventually she ended up in Chicago and married a cultist, and now she spreads the spiritual teachings of the cult and Jupiter on radio talk shows. Nance wipes carob dribbles off her convention schedule. "Look here," she says, "Neva is speaking tomorrow, on the educational system of Jupiter!" "Wowie," I say absently, my eyes trailing Neva as she fades into a far corner of the restaurant, absorbed into a round booth of other higher initiates. She is so glamorous, an iridescent butterfly. I never would have dreamed that in just a few years, I, an ordinary girl from Indiana, a lower initiate, would be living with her ex-husband.

As we return to the convention hotel with its grand circular driveway, excitement is zinging within and without. On the sidewalk in the shade of a palm tree sits a man, an old guy with a beard and shaggy hair. My heart skips a beat, and I nudge Nance, who nods knowingly. Though there is only one living Master, an unbroken line of 972 ascended Masters stretches back to the dawn of life. Ascended Masters can materialize at any time, taking any human form. An ascended Master may even appear as a beggar, in order to test a student. Does the student plow on by or recognize the kindly glint in the beggar's eye? To receive the gaze of a Master is a blessing. A woman in a pale blue dress rushes up to the man, bends down, locks eyes with him, and stuffs a bill in his cup. Then another person approaches, locks eyes with him, stuffs money in his cup; then another, and another. The beggar looks confused, though delighted. Nance says, "Come on," but I shake my head. "Okay, then I'll just go." She digs a dollar out of her patchwork purse, waits until he's free, darts over, bends down, etc. When she returns, she's grinning wildly behind her oval wire rims. She's gained a lot of weight since we've been together, but I like her better this way, with heft to her thighs and ass, her hipbones no longer bruising me. "That was so cool—I could feel this powerful energy emanating from him, like this is the real thing, he even said to me, 'Have a nice day!' And I said to him, 'I will,' and I could tell that he could tell I understood. Dodie, you gotta meet him." "Maybe afterwards," I say. I can now confront salesclerks without trembling, but a Master—I don't know about a Master.

In the hotel ballroom, hundreds of us sit in rows of chairs, facing a stage decorated with a lavish bouquet of yellow gladiolas and a gleaming silver vibraphone. A middle-aged woman leads us in a chant. We close our eyes, and long slow "ahh-ohm"s roll in waves about the room, a lovely harmony of high and low voices, young and old. The energy in the room sparkles, and I feel bathed in love. When I open my eyes, the living Master is sitting beside the gladiolas, on a stool, holding a mic. He's shimmering in his pale blue leisure suit, as if rays of ahh-ohm were emanating from his sleeves. His eyes are small but intense as he surveys the crowd, locking eyes with student after student. Nance was right, we should have gotten here earlier to get closer to the stage. The Master tells us about a single-noted flute he heard on the Soul Plane. "It was very beautifully, hauntingly melodious, uplifting." From that lovely note he realized that it was his spiritual mission to play dinner jazz. "When the words of Man have failed us with the weight of care," he says, "music, which knows no country, race, or creed, gives to each of us according to our need. When used positively—with strings, flutes, vibes, woodwinds, the high notes soft and graceful—it is the speech of God." I look around and notice a preponderance of pale blue leisure suits—and it's not just old guys wearing them—young guys and even little boys rest pale blue polyester arms on the chairbacks of women in pale blue dresses with puffy sleeves. I, in my gauze Indian shirt and hip huggers, think *yuck, how dweeby*—it's like a reflex, my unkind thought, and I flinch at my judgmental attitude. Then I notice this super-cute blond guy across the aisle, with a short beard and Little Dutch Boy haircut. He's wearing his pale blue jacket over a pair of tight white pants. He looks hot, like he could be in the Bee Gees. The Master says, "Divine Love is the binding force of all universes—without it, there would be no life." Nance bites her lower lip and nods slowly, like she's really getting it. She's hugging herself. When she sees me looking at her, she makes a dramatic shiver. It's cold in here. We shiver a lot for each other. It's one of our things. I'm so bored with coupledom. I want adventure, I want to—Dutch Boy crossed his leg, he's wearing platform saddle shoes!—I want to fuck, that's what I want to do, I want to fuck and fuck and fuck my way across the Physical Plane and all the other planes, I want to fuck all the way up to the God Plane. I don't want to be all fat and limited, I want to explode in an orgasm of light and sound. I look up at the Master, he's twirling the cord to his mic; he holds the bulby part close to his mouth, like he's about to lick it. I haven't heard anything he's said— this happens when I play his tapes, but before his powerful incarnate energy I assumed it would be different. His words rush past me in snippets—"sword of God"—"original essence"—"command over the life force"—"divine"—"divine"—"divine"—"divine"—it's like I'm riding in a car on a highway and the Master is as distant as a speck of cow in a field—zoom. Sandy said my inability to take in his words means my conscious mind is not ready for them. She said not to worry, that Soul is listening, drinking in every single nuance. I love being in the cult, I love being privy to the secrets of the universe, I love raising my vibrations, love having the inner Master with me at all times, guiding me in what to eat, how to study, who to love. Once in a dream my Soul rushed from my body—it was a very physical sensation of flying, a blur of colors, yet instantaneous—I found myself in a playground—the Master was standing behind a chain-link fence, smoking a cigarette—I inhaled his sharp toxic fumes and bolted awake in a panic. Cigarettes burn holes in your Astral body. The Master is talking about his life as a jazz musician, how Spirit manifests as light and sound, and dinner jazz is a direct link to the sound of Spirit.

The Sound of Spirit was the name of his album. On it the Master played the vibes and sang about the yearnings of Soul. I listened to it over and over, trying to like it. The lyrics were love songs but instead of being to women, they were to Spirit: "Oh Golden Spirit, I will always love you." On the liner notes it said that the tradition of writing love songs to God is as old as the poetry of Rumi and Kabir. Cult writings always referred to Rumi and Kabir together as if they were a duo like Simon & Garfunkel. The Master sang off-key— perhaps flat is more accurate—and even when expressing spiritual rapture, he warbled without affect. His compositions sounded like they wanted to be in a minor key but couldn't quite get there. The rhythm was slow and draggy like a turntable stuck between speeds. And always the watery boing boing of the vibraphone, which made me think of individual drops of water falling from a tree into a puddle—plop plop boing boing. Maybe some of it was due to the conventions of dinner jazz, which I knew nothing about, but I found the music to be truly awful. I accepted so much—all these wisdom temples and inner worlds; I dutifully memorized the sounds and colors associated with each plane of existence. I believed my female vibratory rate was too coarse for me to be a Master. I believed the rumpled guy sitting outside on the sidewalk was an ascended Master materializing for our spiritual growth; I believed it was against spiritual law to marry outside one's own race; I believed the Holocaust was a learning experience for the Jews, that as Soul each had chosen it as an opportunity to burn off huge amounts of karma quickly. But the Master's record album shook me to the core. How could an enlightened being produce music this bad and not even realize it? So I listened to it every day, waiting and praying for its brilliance to strike me.

Standing up, the Master says, "The type of music to which you listen can have a great effect upon your physical, emotional and mental states. This is why every note I play, sing, write—or chord structure—I try to make it a note of love. This is music that can heal." He pauses, allowing the import of his words to sink in, his blue eyes slowly caressing the crowd. He walks to the edge of the stage and bends down, graciously touching those fortunate enough to be sitting in the first row. Nance nudges me. "Look, it's Sandy!" Yes—the blonde head the Master is patting is wearing an orange smock. I'm surprised I didn't spot her sooner, for the orange really pops out against the tranquil pastels. The Master moves over to the vibraphone and picks up the mallets. "I have a special treat for you, and a special friend is going to help me out with it." From behind the stage steps an attractive woman with long, lustrous chocolate-colored hair that bounces as she walks. It's Anya Grubbs! In her royal blue cocktail dress and matching pumps, she looks ten times more sophisticated than the puffy-sleeved students sitting in floral-printed stackable hotel ballroom chairs. I can't believe I'm seeing Anya Grubbs in the flesh. In a previous incarnation, from 1792 to 1822, she was the poet Shelley. The Master says, "Tomorrow Anya will be reading some of her recent poetry, but tonight she'll be thrilling us with someone else's words. This little melody is about meeting the Master in the inner worlds." As he taps out the opening notes to "Somewhere Over the Rainbow," the room explodes with communal laughter and applause. In a husky voice smooth as malt whiskey, Anya belts out the lyrics: "… there's a land that I heard of once in a lullaby." The Master's blue eyes sparkle and his blue leisure suit slithers around his shoulder as he dramatically raises his arms to strike the vibe. When Anya gets to the line "way above the chimney tops, that's where you'll find me," my eyes water. The cheeks of the women around me—including Nance—are streaming with big alligator tears, and so is that of the blue-suited burly guy in the next row, and the teenage girl beside him. I look across the aisle—yes, Dutch Boy's at it too. I sniffle and sweep my vision across the room. I can't find a single person who isn't weeping. This is the best moment of my entire life, to be a divine tear in an ocean of tenderness for the Master. Anya and the Master lock eyes with the intensity of lovers. Fifteen years later I will learn—surprise—they *were* lovers.

Afterwards, we step outside for some air. Night has fallen, and the palm trees' trunks are wrapped in strands of white Christmas lights. Everything is very clear, like super real, with a peripheral shimmer, Soul is vibrating so intensely. The beggar is still sitting on the sidewalk. Dollar bills in hand, students are approaching in a steady stream. I'm so high from "Somewhere Over the Rainbow," I join the line. Nance waits with me. She's wearing her favorite corduroy jeans, a soft faded coral. "I feel like going up to him again," she says, "but I don't want to be greedy. Hey, Dodie, look at his cup!" The afternoon's coin cup has been replaced by a 2 pound coffee can that's overflowing with bills. I imagine a gust of wind and all that Dāna twirling down the street like crumpled green leaves. The man pays no heed to the money as he sits there soaking up our love. "He no longer needs to beg," says Nance. "He's like the lilies of the field." The blue-skirted astrology duo swoop in on either side of him, graceful as swans. In unison they kiss his cheeks. The scraggly Master gives the crowd a thumbs up, and everybody laughs and applauds. I zone in on the palm tree I'm standing beside, tiny white lights spiraling its trunk like fairy kisses. It's massive. I have to bend my head way back to see the fronds. I caress the pineappley bark. It emits powerful energy. I've always been struck by the energy of trees. The last time we dropped acid—which was like two years ago, we don't do drugs in the cult— Nance couldn't get me out of the meadow beside the student union building, so mesmerized was I by the cool shimmering emanations of the ancient oaks. She's sure I was a Druid in a former life. Finally it's my turn. "I'm so glad you're doing this," Nance says as I step towards the man. Everybody's watching me; my legs are fat blobs of wobbly jello. When I bend down with my money, I smell alcohol urine rancid sweat. The man stares at the sidewalk and mumbles, "Thanks." No gaze, no blessing, just this stinky old guy raking in cash. On my heels is a woman with a little blonde girl, both of them wearing puffy sleeved blue dresses, both of them waving dollar bills. "Mommy, mommy, look at the Master!"

Later that evening when Nance and I make out in the king-sized hotel bed, I imagine I'm peeling off Dutch Boy's baby blue jacket and tight white pants. His body is tawny, his cock pink and eager. I leave on the platform saddle shoes. As I hump my clit against Nance's thigh, Dutch Boy whispers in a low growl, "Let me take you over the rainbow."

The cult taught us to leave our bodies—you sit or lie down, close your eyes, and focus on your third eye, that spot in the center of your forehead. You look for light, listen for the sounds of other planes—*flutes rushing water buzzing of bees, etc.* Mostly I waited and fidgeted until the time was up. I did leave my body, but not during my daily meditations. It usually happened in the mornings before the alarm went off. When leaving my body felt good, it was a whooshing through space, blink blink zoom zoom I'm across the room, blink zoom I'm soaring through the sky looking down at the ground. These experiences were dreamlike, for sure, but also very real. Super-real. When I left my body and stayed earthbound, that's when it felt bad. I'd be lying in bed, suddenly conscious but unable to wake up, unable to move. Trapped in this leaden, immobilized carcass, I strain to roll over, to lift a finger, and the more I try the more I'm overtaken with a dull, thick anxiety. Several struggling minutes later, I manage to separate from my body and stand beside the bed; my vision is blurred, and it's terribly dim, as if the pink chenille curtains have absorbed all the light in the room. I don't have a lot of control over my body, so I jerk-walk over to the light switch. When I try to flick it on, my hand goes right through the switch, and I try again, and I keep trying, over and over, swiping my hand across the switch with a limp-wristed flail—but I am never able to turn on the light. This must be how ghosts feel, frustrated and frightened. The demon fucking begins the same way. I'm suddenly conscious, lying on my back, being fucked—at first I think it's my boyfriend, but then I remember he didn't spend the night, that I slept alone—I can't bring it into focus, this presence slamming away inside me—smear of motion like a Francis Bacon painting—not human—a cold mechanized malevolence that lurches my body— but I cannot move this Dodie body myself, no matter how much I struggle I cannot move, cannot push the grunting thing away. Not just its cock, its entire body is hard, like I'm being fucked by rigor mortis. This happened many times—in Indiana and in California, on a mattress on the floor and in an antique inlaid mahogany bed. It never happened before I joined the cult, and it hasn't happened since I left, yet I never associated these experiences with the cult, for they were negative, and the cult was obsessively positive. Towards the end, in the early 80s when I was struggling to leave, I started smoking grass and for the first time in my life felt a terror of embodiment—all the proportions were wrong and I staggered across the kitchen, feeling like I was shrinking. I stopped smoking grass, but the terror continued. I'd be at work and suddenly the alienness of my body would hit me in a blast of panic, and my boss's movements would look jagged, like a poorly-rendered animation, and I'd desperately be trying to act normal.

My tenth year in the cult, my Master was excommunicated. He was a fallen master, I was told, because he had held on to the Wand of God too long, and it burned him. My Master got so drunk, I was told, he had to be hauled back to his hotel room. Not just once, many times. My Master was a womanizer. He embezzled 2.5 million cult dollars. In order to avoid paying California sales tax on the private executive jet he bought to transport his band on its spiritual dinner jazz tours, he funneled funds into a secret corporation he'd started in Oregon, and now the California State Board of Equalization was after my cult. My Master was ousted with no pension, severance pay, or compassion—through continuous litigation he was drained of all his money—and his name was erased from cult history. The new Master is not charismatic like my Master. He's mousy and repressed. With swords of jealousy, hate, envy and greed, he has annihilated my Master. The new Master threatened cultists with loss of initiation and expulsion should they attempt to communicate with my Master, and he replaced my Master's teachings with benign, feel-good, New Age drivel. The new Master claimed my Master was a black magician, and he warned students not to open any letters from my Master, for opening such a letter would trigger a post-hypnotic suggestion. The new Master instructed students to destroy all my Master's materials. The fear and confusion instilled in these Souls was ugly and terrifying. Witness the following, from a cult survivors forum: *There had been a raffle of some of the Master's possessions: one of his vibraphones, a xylophone, and some other things. Well I was shocked to be selected to receive the xylophone! I so enjoyed hearing the sounds of the instrument at home, using it for contemplation. But then, after the Master was excommunicated and portrayed as the Black Magician, I followed the instructions to destroy anything written by or owned by the old Master. Reluctantly but dutifully, I carried out a plan to dismantle the xylophone, note by note, and, fearing someone would somehow re-assemble it, drove around to every dumpster in the county and placed each wrapped piece in a different one.* The new Master's mind-numbed minions hurled my Master's book and tapes into backyard bonfires or dumped them into the Chicago River. In Europe, $40,000 worth of my Master's scriptures were burnt in an official cult incinerator. Even though he has god awareness, my Master didn't know about all the intrigue going on behind his back because no Master can dwell in total awareness all the time unless someone takes care of the body, washes it from head to toe, feeds it, as devotees fed and washed Krishna. My Master has developed the ability to be in total awareness for up to forty-five minutes to an hour at a time. My Master says that those individuals concerned about psychic attacks and black magicians should know that Spirit is stronger than any negative force. The dark force does not like the light. My Master has the backing of the ascended Masters, and no words, spoken or on a piece of paper, can change that.

1977. Nance and I, still together, are in grad school. I have no interest in grad school, but I would have done anything to get out of the dorm cafeteria. Sandy's left, and the Bloomington chapter of the cult is led by Clark and Joanne, a trust fund couple who own a farm outside of town. They make beautiful stained glass windows, which they sell at crafts fairs. Sometimes they give Nance and me fresh goat milk and eggs. I learn that goat milk varies from drinkable to yuck depending on what the goats have been eating. Break Your Fast Sizzler-fest is still going strong. One Friday evening, when it's just me and Nance and this married couple we're always with, Bob and Susie, I suggest we head over to a pop-up disco I've heard about. "It's in a loft near campus, and Troy says they have a really good sound system, and the line dancing is a blast!" The place is packed with lines of dancers twenty college students wide; there are several rows of them, all moving in unison to Thelma Houston's "Don't Leave Me This Way." Dust motes swirl in the light of a revolving overhead silver ball. When the song ends, we dart into the mass of bodies and squeeze in between whoever will make room for us. Having major body-image issues and no rhythm, I've always been terrified of dancing in public, but here I feel safe, ensconced in the center of a block of bodies, everybody facing the same direction, foot forward, foot back, tap, tap, kick, turn, a dance as formulaic as a badly executed sonnet; people keep fucking up and laughing about it, "Love to love you, baby," nobody is looking at me, nobody cares when I have to scamper in some extra baby steps to get back in the groove. Afterwards, as we walk home through the jasmine-scented streets, Bob is so excited he exclaims, "We should do this in Indianapolis!" The Bloomington chapter of the cult is scheduled to give a performance at the upcoming regional symposium, but nobody has yet come up with a plan. "Great idea," I chime in with Nance, knowing that Bob will wrest control and drive me crazy. I can't stand Bob, but he's Nance's best friend. He got drafted but somehow managed to spend the Vietnam War in an office in Florida, drinking and having a nervous breakdown—that's the kind of guy he is, always working the system. It's his goal to climb the ranks of the cult—he actually said to me, "I want a position of leadership in the cult"—and so he's always chumming it up with the middle-aged housewives who run the state; he yucks it up with them like he was their best girlfriend. He's a real closet type—his apartment is decorated in glass and chrome, and once when he and Susie had us over for dinner they fixed chicken pot pie from a recipe in *TV Guide*. Because of Nance, he and I tolerate each other, barely. As we cross Kirkwood Avenue, Bob says, "And I can direct the whole thing. I'm good at that."

We gathered sixteen students, which was practically the entire Bloomington chapter, to participate. This was the minimum needed to form a tight block: four rows wide, four rows deep. Bob also enlisted one flute player, Mary, this odd woman who would randomly burst into hysterical laughter. We learned the steps to the Bus Stop and practiced and practiced. Bob—short dirty blond shag—was impatient and tyrannical, like a Jerome Robbins in training. "Left, move your foot left! Don't you know your left from your right?" "You look like a ragged mess—keep in formation!"

Whenever Bob yelled, Mary let loose a full-lunged, high-pitched cackle. Bob ignored her, but it was clear she was getting to him, and finally he shouted, "Shut—the—fuck—up!" "Language," Clark said to him. "That language isn't suitable for cult gatherings." Mary shrieked giddily. "Sorry," Bob mumbled. When performing the kick steps, people kept striking the person in front of them, or wobbling and grabbing on to one another. "No more kicks," Bob said. "You look like a bunch of spazzes. We can do the Bus Stop without kicks." Our uniform was non-jean bell bottoms and button-down shirts. At first Bob insisted on matching shirts, but we were poor students and we rebelled. "Why can't we just wear shirts we already have!" "Whatever," huffed Bob, "but it won't look as good."

At the symposium, Mary stands offstage with her flute, as the rest of us form our four-by-four block. Over the loudspeakers blares "Boogie Down USA," chosen for its heavy beat and minimal vocals. In unison we perform a robotic Bus Stop, arms straight down at our sides, fists clenched, legs stiff, our faces void of emotion, stomping forward then back, right then left, double tap forward, double tap back, turn. We represent the confines of humdrum life on the Physical Plane. The volume is slowly lowered on "Boogie Down USA" until the pure, sweet notes of Mary's flute can be heard. The flute is the sound of the Soul Plane. One by one, starting with students on the outside of the block, we cup our hands to our ears and look surprised as we hear the flute, and then we start swaying, and step out of the block, and twirl about, flailing our arms in fluid freeform movement. "Boogie Down USA" continues to fade until all that is heard is Mary's flute and all sixteen of us are slithering around the stage, waving our arms, throwing our heads skyward, dropping our jaws and bugging our eyes in an approximation of inspired ecstasy. This is Soul breaking out of the conformity of the lower worlds. The performance, as cheesy as it was, felt like a metaphor for my own desperate boredom—Nance and I had become one dull being with four legs, trudging from potluck to group discussion to literature table to chewy steak dinner. I had no friends of my own; I hadn't even cheated on her for a couple of years. I was imploding from claustrophobia. In the fall, when we moved to Chicago, I was determined I would finally break out.

Nance and I found a shabby, high-ceilinged flat a few blocks from the Lake, in New Town, a funky, queer neighborhood with boy hustlers hanging out on the corner of Clark and Broadway. Nance commuted to an instructional development position in Joliet, where the prison is, and I enrolled in the photography program at the Institute of Design, where I learned I was better at looking at pictures than taking them. I dropped out after a semester and found a job as a photographer's assistant at the corporate office of Montgomery Ward, the city's signature department store. I helped with tabletop setups of shoes, etc. I was not very good at this as I could not see how this bit needed a fill light, but this bit didn't. I also shot slides on the copy stand, burning "Ward's Best" into the blank space beside the shoes. For fun, I duped a photograph of myself, a three-quarter profile with my hair pulled back into a bushy pony tail, and I burned "Ward's Best" next to my crooked grin. Nance and I spent every evening together, every second of the weekend together, mostly running errands. My claustrophobia raged to the point that I'd occasionally call in sick, just to have a few glorious hours alone. To make matters worse, Bob and Susie followed us to Chicago, installing their glass and chrome furniture into a high rise with a view of the Lake, and they became our entire social life, save for an occasional cult meeting. At the cult center I practically peed my pants when handed a flyer for a class, "The Secret Gospels of Primeval Prophecy," taught by Ned Novak— the former husband of Neva, the woman from Jupiter! I'd seen him once before, at our Indianapolis regional symposium. He was the keynote speaker. As I twirled about the stage, a Soul freed from "Boogie Down USA" conformity, I noticed him in the audience, in the front row, close enough to reach out and grab my ankle. He was roaring with laughter, his deep-set eyes sparkling. To prepare for his class I went on the Master Cleanse, subsisting on lemonade made with maple syrup and cayenne. After three days my blood sugar was so low I almost fainted at work and they sent me home, but I kept cleansing.

I arrive at Primeval Prophecy, weak from hunger, high from sugar, cheeks flushed from cayenne, stomach flat as it's ever been. Eight of us sit on folding chairs in a semi-circle facing Ned, who overwhelms a dilapidated sofa, massive legs crossed, long arms outstretched on the sofa back. Full head of wavy, dark brown hair. "Do not confuse the cult's system of prophecy with fortune telling," he begins. "The vibrations of anyone practicing Primeval Prophecy are so high," he says, "that those on the lower psychic scale can never be compared with them. But I'm getting ahead of myself!" He lets out a deep-throated laugh. "Let's back up and do some intros." "I just moved here from Bloomington," I say. "Bloomington! I thought you looked familiar. Were you part of the controversial Soul disco?" As I murmur yes, he laughs again, blue eyes peering at me from beneath his bushy unibrow, intense icy blue eyes. "The notice headquarters sent out about no disco dancing at symposiums was a total overreaction. So what are you doing here in Chi-Town?" "I work as a photographer's assistant, but really I'm a poet." "You'll have to show me some of your poetry sometime. I'm an artist. I have a studio in Old Town." He peers into me like I'm the only person in the room—he's that intense. Nance scoots her chair an inch closer to mine and clears her throat. "What's your name?" Ned asks her, but he keeps looking at me. Once the intros are through, we all sit with our spines straight and chant ah-ohm for a few minutes. Adepts in the Khachöpelri Monastery in Northern Tibet are the custodians of the secret gospels of Primeval Prophecy. Not even the Dalai Lama knows about the gospels because they are higher than his level of consciousness. Primeval Prophecy was also practiced by the oracle of Ancient Greece, whose temple now lies in ruins. Primeval Prophecy works by means of an instant projection of consciousness which transcends time, space, energy, and matter, to the Soul Plane. From this height, the readings of an individual, a nation, or the universe are taken.

When I open my eyes, the energy has shifted. We students smile sweetly at one another, the Soul in each of us vibrating in harmony. Ned no longer singles me out. He's a conduit of Spirit, and a conduit of

Spirit would not be flirting during an official cult meeting. He teaches with an easy confidence. Our cult has been around since the dawn of time, he says. Over 30,000 years ago, our cult was being taught in Egypt in its pure form—the Egyptian government has evidence to prove this, but they're withholding it. We shuffle in our folding chairs, shocked. "Why would Egypt do that?" "Because agents of the negative force hold high positions of power there." Our cult has been battling the negative force through all the stages of mankind—the Golden Age, the Bronze Age, the Iron Age, and especially now, in the Kali Yuga, the worst age. Eventually everything will fall apart and the world will end, take a long sleep, and then the whole cycle will begin all over again—the Masters know this because they can read the future, which is inscribed in the higher planes. This class is going to teach us how to utilize Primeval Prophecy to become clearer channels in the fight against the negative force. "All paths are valid," Ned says, changing the topic without transition, "each created for the level of consciousness of its age. Jesus Christ was a member of our cult, but he only progressed to the second level of initiation, because that's where the consciousness of his age was at." "Jesus Christ, really?" "Yes, really." Our cult is the most direct path to god—Ned uncrosses his massive legs and sits upright—and we mustn't study other paths because their lower vibrations will—Ned enunciates the words slowly and with conviction—"slow—down—your—spiritual—growth." Particularly dangerous is kundalini yoga, where they zap energy from the base of the spine upwards and out the top of the head. Should we try this—he furls his bushy unibrow and scans our semi-circle, locking eyes with each of us in turn—when he gets to Nance, she looks away—should we try this, he repeats, we could end up psychotic or worse. "You should only move energy downward," he warns. "Close your eyes, place your palms in your lap, left palm over right, loosely opened, facing upward. Now envision golden energy entering your crown chakra and gently moving down your spine. See how good that feels? Keep moving the golden energy downward. Allow the light of Spirit to completely fill you." In Bloomington one of the cultists, Carl, was dating a girl into kundalini yoga, Pam—and she told me all these amazing experiences she had zapping energy upward. Pam was an artist, and her studio was in a corn silo. She told me about tantric sex, too, and I got a book, and I wondered if that was why Carl was so into her. A couple of times when I was cheating on Nance and the guy was taking forever, I imagined pulling the energy of his cock into my cunt and up my spine—and—zap!—the guy comes like crazy. I felt powerful, ecstatic—even though I wasn't coming in my physical body, it was like I was coming *somewhere,* in another body on a higher plane. "Only move the energy downward," Ned intones, looking directly at me. Sternly. He's a sixth initiate: of course he can read my secret pervert heresies like a book. "If you move the energy in any other direction it will screw you up." I nod at him sheepishly, and the corners of his mouth curl, almost imperceptivity, into a grin. When I leave, he yells after me, "See you on the inner!"

When Ned told me that the last woman he slept with smoked a cigarette afterwards, I was shocked he'd be intimate with someone whose Astral body was ravaged. He hung his head, desperation leaking from his wolf eyes, and I reached out to him with tender, smokefree fingers. He was a cab driver, and for our second date, he picked me up in his cab at 5 a.m. and drove us to Lake Michigan to watch the sun rise over the water. Golden beams of morning kissed our kissing faces. The Lake shimmered like a liquid jewel; gulls squawked like angels. We were blessed and anything seemed possible. When I got home Nance threw me out, and I moved in with him. Ned's apartment was in New Town, which in the 60s was the Greenwich Village of Chicago. In high school Nance and I took the train up from Indiana one afternoon to immerse ourselves in the hippies. In Piper's Alley we ate a deep dish pizza served by a waitress in a flowing floorlength skirt worn over a black leotard, hair pulled back into a low bun, huge hoops in her ears, a look I would never tire of copying. We bought incense and love beads and fringed suede shoulder bags, and in a head shop I found a poster of Allen Ginsberg, a grainy black-and-white headshot. So I was walking down Wells Street with the rolled-up poster under my arm, imagining how great it would look on my bedroom wall, when some scraggly guy sitting on the sidewalk pointed to it and yelled, "Tourists, go back to where you came from!" I hurried across the street, eyes tearing. I'm not a tourist anymore, I thought, as Ned and I hauled boxes of my stuff up the stairs to his backyard cottage, which was built above a garage. With my Teacher/sixth initiate boyfriend, high in the air, surrounded by treetops and light, life from then on would be one long spiritual retreat; I'd be like one of those ancient naked yogis who lives on a platform on stilts, wooden fence all around to hide his enlightened cock and balls as he waves to his devotees.

We settled into an easy, ecstatic domesticity. I cooked for him; I met his friends, his family; I drove with him in his baby blue VW van to Michigan to a reunion of the folk music camp he went to as a kid. See a splurge of green, leaf-heavy trees everywhere, happy happy people sitting on the grass, group-singing to a gaggle of strumming guitars. Ned joined the band for a couple of numbers, playing his recorder. As his fingers throbbed along the wooden stick in his mouth, he smiled at me, only at me, with his intense blue eyes. He was so handsome he was epic. The camp promoted social justice and racial equality. Pete Seeger used to teach there. This was a different Michigan from the one I grew up with. In high school my mother would drive me to a fat-doctor in Michigan, just one county over from the camp. The clinic was boxy and cheap; it reminded me of the vet clinic where I took my cat Molly for low-cost spaying, especially with the cattle scale in the waiting room for the really large women. My mom and I, and usually a couple of her friends, would each get weighed, thankfully on human scales, and if you hadn't lost enough weight, the doctor would amp up your prescription of Dexedrine. When I went away to college, the doctor would mail the pills to me. I studied like a maniac; I found studying to be glorious; my heart grew sloppy over geography and Chaucer. Nance was addicted to them too, even though she wasn't fat. When we joined the cult and learned that drugs put holes in your Astral body, we both went through a painful detox. I became a listless, bored student. Ned was the first red diaper baby I ever met. He was raised in Oak Park, where they have all the Frank Lloyd Wright houses. When I visited his childhood home, my jaw dropped. The house was cool and dim, flooded with oxygen from the massive trees that surrounded it. The oak floors were strewn with Bokharas. In the living room a dark wooden bookcase took up an entire wall, and it was filled with hardbacks and other quality material. On the other walls hung tribal masks and oil paintings by local artists. Above the dining room table, a mobile that Ned had made himself twirled slowly. It was comprised of blobby shapes cut from cardboard, painted with day-glo acrylic, and hung from twisted coat hangers. "See how the air moves between the forms?" "Yes," I said, "it's like a ballet." "That's Spirit directing their movements." He wrapped his arm around my waist and pulled me to his body. He was tall and sturdy as a door frame yet so sensitive he choreographed Spirit. My heart felt open, really, really open; I could weep from such openness. Ned had been the luckiest kid on earth, to be raised without wall-to-wall sculpted beige carpeting, to spend the summers in a lefty arts camp, to have parents who discussed *issues*. His mother was a feminist and I adored her.

When Ned asked me if I wanted to drive down to Tennessee to visit his ex-wife Neva, I jumped at the chance. Five years before, when I joined the cult, Neva was famous, but no one seemed to mention her anymore. I thought back to my first national convention, where she spoke about the education system on Jupiter, how dazzling she looked with her platinum bangs cut ruler straight and her lips a stop-sign red. She wore white head to foot, a tight sheath skirt topped with a short fringed poncho with holes cut out at the collarbone and shoulders. Neva was raised on the Astral Plane, and on the Astral Plane there is no commerce, no need to work. Instead of religious temples, the temples on Ganymede are devoted to learning, with each temple dedicated to a specific aspect of the arts or sciences. Children have complete freedom to study in any temple of their choice. Neva's favorite temple was dance, and I had heard that back in the days when the first Western Master was alive, she would perform Jovian dances at national conventions. In the cult we were taught that by raising our vibratory rate we could travel to these learning temples on the Etheric Plane, that these temples contained all knowledge—present, past, and future—and that great inventors or artists, such as Beethoven, traveled to these temples and brought back their discoveries. This book, *The TV Sutras,* exists in perfect form in a temple of learning, and its success depends not on how good a writer I am, but on how efficient I am at channeling the perfect book from the Etheric Plane.

After much gunning of the engine, Ned's baby blue van finally starts, and we're on our way. Whenever we stop at a gas station, it dies, and there's more frantic gunning. Stop lights are usually okay, but sometimes it dies at them as well. "When we get back I've got to get this thing fixed." My pea-sized bladder becomes a big issue. "But, Ned, I can't hold it any longer!" "If we stop the van will die." "I'll run in real quick and you can keep it on idle." "It doesn't like to idle." Finally he'd pull over somewhere and drive the van in circles while I gushed out urine and ran after him. As we wound our way southward, Ned told me how he met Neva. It was the late 60s. He was walking down a street in Old Town, and this beautiful red-headed woman leaned out a window and shot him with a pretend bow and arrow. Ned grasped his chest, staggered, and fell to the ground. He steers the van with one hand, his left elbow poking out the window. There'sno air conditioning and it's like 200 degrees in the South and humid as hell. "Neva was wild in those days." Ned laughs and shakes his head. "She was a barmaid, and she would wear this skintight leopardskin bodysuit to work, and when a song she liked came on the jukebox, she'd jump on a table and go-go dance, flinging her arms and hips. She made tips like crazy. It's like she could just look at a guy and he'd empty his pockets for her." Soon afterwards the two of them joined the cult and were welcomed into the Master's inner circle. Online I find a picture of Neva with the first Western Master. The year is 1971. She's very Jane Asher with her mane of bright strawberry hair softly pulled back, single loose banana curl on either side, gold velvet choker around her neck. She's so beautiful, it's shocking. Her eyes are locked with the Master's, a sacred rite for the cultist. The Master's gaze looks flirtatious, his face lit up and smirking like a man besotted. I pull out the front of my tank top and shake it, to create a breeze on my sticky chest. "So how long were you guys together?" "Ten years." "Why'd you break up?" "We decided to just be friends," Ned says quickly and without affect, like he's delivered these exact words many times. He pauses for a bit then adds, "Who wants a Jupiterian wife who dances on tables." Neva published a memoir, *Jovial I Am*, frequented latenight radio talk shows and was well on her way to becoming a prominent extraterrestrial, but then she inexplicably moved back to Tennessee with her mother.

At the end of a bumpy, unpaved road, we stop at what is little more than a shack. No grass in the front yard, just dried weeds and crumbly dirt. The screen door opens, and Neva emerges, barefooted with stringy hair. She sits down on the distressed wooden steps and waves at us with the cigarette in her right hand. She's wearing a sundress the color of faded denim. It swims on her. Ned says, "Neva, are you okay?" She takes a drag off her cigarette and says, "Yeah, I'm fine." Behind her a slight, hunch-shouldered woman rushes down the stairs and into Ned's arms. He gives her a bear hug and she says, "I'm always happy to see my favorite son-in-law." "Ex-son-in-law," he corrects. "Ned, you'll never be ex in my heart." She's wearing tan walking shorts and a sleeveless blouse patterned with little lavender flowers. "This is Neva's mother, Reva," Ned says to me. "Nice to meet you." She grasps my hand like it's a treasure. Even though she's really old, like 50, her hands are soft. "Nice to meet you too, darlin'," she says. I try not to stare at her missing front tooth. Her graying hair is pulled back into a low ponytail, which really accentuates the tooth hole. "You all must be bushed from such a long ride," the not-tooth says. "Come on inside, I'll make you all a nice glass of sweet tea." Reva leads us up the porch, her flipflops flapping against the bottoms of her feet. Inside, Ned looms in the small, low-ceilinged living room. Reva says, "Neva, run in the kitchen and fetch a couple of chairs." Ned says, "I can get them." "No, no, Neva can handle it, you rest." "I insist," Ned says.

All three of them disappear into the kitchen, and I examine the framed photos hanging behind the sofa. In the middle of the usual mixture of school and wedding and bowling team portraits is an 8 x 10 sepia-toned headshot of a surprisingly sophisticated young woman. She's got teased bangs, shaped brows, and eyeliner so perfectly applied that a machine could have etched it, and she's wearing a simple scoop-necked dress, with a sheen to the fabric. No jewelry. She doesn't need it. She looks more mid-60s Carnaby Street than Tennessee. Her eyes are smiling, but her lips don't quite get there. The dimples on either side of her mouth look cramped. I touch a finger to the portrait's wide full lips and think, there's a fine line between a smile and a grimace. "You like that photo?" Reva says. The kitchen team has returned with tea and a couple of vinyl chairs. "That's Neva's high school graduation picture. Her grandma made that dress for her. Her grandmother was always making her dresses from the scraps left over from her sewing clients. When Neva was in grade school I counted, and she had twenty-seven dresses. Even though we was dirt poor, Neva had more dresses than any of the other girls at school." Neva sits down on one of the vinyl chairs and rolls her eyes. Reva says, "Here, Ned, sit on the sofa beside me." "That's okay, a chair's fine for me. Dodie can have the sofa," says Ned, a bit too gallantly.

I move aside a cross-stitched pillow and join Reva on the liver-colored velvet sofa. It smells like patchouli and ashtray. We sip our sweet tea as Reva and Ned swap platitudes. "You know, Reva, a journey of a thousand miles begins with a single step." "You are so right, Ned. The river always runs one way, and it always goes to something bigger, so just roll with the current instead of against it." I watch

Neva smoke. She has her legs crossed, exposing her knees. The elbow of her cigarette arm is propped on her thigh. When she takes a drag, her arm remains stationary as the wrist hinges towards her mouth, then back again. An economical movement. She's looking above our heads, at her high school portrait on the wall. Ned says, "My van isn't going to roll anywhere if I don't get it checked out when we get back to Chicago." Reva leans over and taps the Bible sitting on the pineapple-doilied end table. "I knew you was gonna say that!" "Reva is psychic," Ned explains. "I knew you was gonna say that as well!" Ned laughs. "Neva, she's got the gift too," Reva continues. "Ever since she was a little whip, she's been answering questions before they was asked. Her teachers sayed they never see'd nothing like it. Right Neva?" "What?" "Your teachers, they was scared of you." "Oh. Yeah." Neva shoos a fly with her cigarette hand and vacantly stares at the scratches in the brown enameled wooden floor. Ned says, "Neva, are you sure you're all right?" Neva glares at him, then sighs and takes a deep suck from her Marlboro Menthol, exhaling the smoke through her nostrils. Reva says, "Neva's been a bit under the weather, but she's a-mending. Neva was always sickly. When she was a baby she was so scrawny her little intestines showed right through her skin. I was only fourteen when I had her. I didn't know nothin' 'bout raising a baby. But my Neva, she turned out all right. She's been on national TV. If I was half as bad a mother as them welfare people sayed I was, my little darlin' wouldn't have growed up to go on national TV. Right?" Ned nods in agreement. Neva flashes me a sly smile and says, "So you and my boy Ned here, are you having fun?" This is the first time she's acknowledged my presence. "Yeah, sure, we're having lots of fun." She picks a piece of tobacco from her lower lip and says flatly, "Enjoy it while it lasts." Despite her hollow cheeks, the bags under her eyes, the patch of acne beside her mouth, the rooty bleached hair, Neva is still striking. I imagine her on the wall beside her high school portrait, desperate and grainy and more beautiful because of it. I blurt out what I've been dying to ask ever since we arrived. "How are things on Jupiter?" "I don't talk about Jupiter any more."

Jupiter is certainly sexier than rural Tennessee. As a young child, Neva was severely malnourished, with chronic diarrhea and infected ears and throat. Her stepdaddy was a mean son of a bitch, but handsome as the day was long, and charming. According to Reva, "He could talk a man outta his last nickel." When Neva was seven, stepdaddy tried to strangle her, so she was sent alone on a bus to live in a housing project with her grandmother. The bus crashed, killing Earth Neva, and she was replaced by a 212-year-old Jovian who looked just like her. The grandmother had sugar diabetes, and so many tumors on her stomach she looked eight months pregnant. When I was a child, I too developed a fantasy character, this supergirl named Sally, who eventually permutated to Sandy—and yes, it is an amazing coincidence that the person who brought me into the cult had the same name as my fantasy figure—that's her real name—and Sandy the cultist was in many ways similar to my inner Sandy, beautiful and bigger than life. In my imaginary realm, Sally or Sandy would relive the plots of favorite TV shows, tweaked to star her—it was not some sixties starlet but Sandy who sat between Buzz and Todd as they sped down Route 66 in a Corvette. Dodie never entered my fantasy narratives. She didn't deserve to be in them. This continued through high school, and it was my biggest secret, even bigger than the sex with Nance, that I spent much of my free time pretending to be another. Like Neva, if I had had the opportunity to step out of my shitty childhood and into the body a better, more exotic girl, I would have dumped this lump called Dodie in a minute. When I joined the cult I no longer needed a dream world, no longer needed a glamorous avatar, for I was Soul and Soul is the most beautiful.

When we get into the van, Ned groans, "That was depressing." "What happened to her?" "I don't know, I don't want to talk about it." "How long has she been like this?" "I said I don't want to talk about it!" Ned's van barely made it back to Chicago in one piece. It needed a shitload of work and he didn't have the funds to fix it—but he was using the As If Principle to attract the money. According to the As If Principle, if you want something in your life, you act as if you already have it. While he looks at the road I look at his sweaty profile—angular as an Easter Island head—or a superhero—and I have my first pang of *who is this guy, what am I doing here.* It's not that I wasn't prepared for the As If Principle. Pyramid schemes and their positive thinking ideology were rampant in the cult. Cultists dreamed of being self-supporting, anything to avoid the nine-to-five grind. And who can blame them? I teach creative writing, fully aware it is as much a racket as selling vitamins formulated by the first Western Master's wife. I finger the van's frayed baby blue upholstery and ask, "So, do you just wait for the money to just appear—or do you have, like, a plan?" "Of course I have a plan, Grasshopper! I'm manifesting someone to buy one of my mobiles. But first I had to clear away my psychological blocks to success, and that's been fantastic, the clearing. My mobiles have never received the attention they deserve." I nod. "Yeah, they're great." "So, at first I was trying to manifest someone to pay me $5,000 for one. And then I said to myself, 'Why set your sights so low? Why not ask for $50,000?' It's not unheard of for a piece of art to go for that much, right?" I nod. He takes his right hand from the wheel and sweeps it in a wide arc. "Why fix this piece of junk when I could manifest the money for a new one?" The pitch of his voice is rising, the way it does when he gets hyper-excited. Now he's banging the dashboard, shouting, "I can do this, all I have to do is manifest the material prosperity that reflects the spiritual abundance I already have!" Ned knows a couple of people who show in local galleries, but up until now has eschewed such connections, wanting to keep his art pure. I remember him telling me, "I could have made a killing in the portrait business but I felt like a prostitute. The energy of capitalism just isn't me." Like many of us, he trained in pastel portraiture with Sandy's mother, Pat. The portrait he's most proud of is an impressionistic, lopsided Neva, above her head an arc of colorful planets and stars. Once when we were in a cafe eating Eggs Benedict (his favorite) he sketched me on a napkin. A cartoon woman with messy slashes for bangs. "But it doesn't look like me," I blurted out stupidly. "Why do you always have to be so negative," he said, crumbling the napkin. "It's you on the inner." We hit a bump in the road and my bladder lurches. "Ned, I'm sorry, but I gotta pee." "Okay, okay. I saw a sign for McDonalds.

When I get my new van, you can pee as often as you like, you can pee day and night." We both laugh, then he adds, "You should try the As If Principle yourself. To get rid of some of that weight."

Ned's bedroom is teeny, the bed filling most of the space like a sleeper car, which makes sex feel womblike. He lifts his head from between my legs and says, "Your pussy tastes better than any other pussy I've tried." He's such a kind, sensitive lover, the way he makes me feel special. "Yum yum," he says, "and now it's time for me to put my yang in your yoni." I giggle and wiggle my hips, and he dives in, laughing. He's 35, by far the oldest person I've fucked. He's so old that sometimes he can't keep it up and other times it takes him forever to climax. I've never had an orgasm with a guy and I've kind of given that up as an expectation. With Nance I could come in the blink of an eye. I look up at him, panting and banging away, how long has it been, ten minutes, twenty, a year, and I consider my ability to pull energy up my spine and zap men into orgasm, but then I remember Ned's warning in Primeval Prophecy: *Only move the energy downward.* The veins on his forehead are bulging *downward downward* he's turning beet red he's straining he's going to slam my head into the wall *downward* I'm getting raw I can't stand it *downward downward downward* I whoosh the energy from my yoni up my spine, like I'm a vacuum sucking the cum right out of him *you're going to pay for this, the negative powers are going to shoot up through you and into him and you'll both end up in the back ward of a mental hospital, drooling and humping chairs* he lets out a roar and spasms. "That was amazing," he says.

Molly, my temperamental, high-strung calico, has not been happy with our move to New Town. In Bloomington she roamed the neighborhood freely—when we would throw balls of crumpled aluminum foil, she'd jump up and do somersaults in the air—but now she's stuck in a cramped apartment with an enclosed thumbnail of a yard and this new 6'2" hulk of a roommate who doesn't smell anything like Nance. She struggles whenever Ned picks her up, she cries constantly and scratches the furniture—and now she's peed on the throw pillow on the couch. Cross-stitched with the cult's blue and yellow bullseye logo, the pillow is Ned's most prized possession. A look of rage crosses his face as he clamps a corner of the damp uriney thing between his thumb and pointer finger, and raises it in the air. "That cat did this on purpose. That cat's out to get me." Molly has always been wickedly perceptive. In Bloomington, she would follow us to campus, which at first we thought was cool, but, invariably, half way there she'd freak out and scamper up a tree and wouldn't come down. We resorted to sneaking away from the house when she wasn't around, but Molly would come running after us, out of nowhere, and we'd stand on the sidewalk impotently yelling, "Go home! Go home!" Whenever we held a cult class in our living room, just as it was about to begin she'd come in from outside and take a seat on my lap. "Look, she came to satsang again. She's studying the discourses too!" Bloomington cultists joked about which level of initiation she had attained. "Neva's mother made this for me," Ned says, his unibrow furled in rage. "And now because of you and your cat, it's ruined." "Come on, Ned, I didn't pee on it. I'm sorry." Ned takes a deep breath, slowly walks across the room, opens the screen door, and drops the pillow on the porch. When he returns, the rage had been wiped from his face. "Sorry, I'm being silly. The pillow's just a trinket of the material world. Soul is what matters. And you of course." He makes a goofy little smile and opens his arms. "Come here." As we stand there embracing, his chin resting on the top of my head, he says, "But that cat, Dodie, I don't know if I can deal with that cat."

Molly went to live with Nance, but tensions between Ned and me escalated. He was spending more and more time at his studio. He couldn't think, having me around all the time, he'd grumble, and he'd take off. He'd return several hours later, sullen because he'd slept all afternoon instead of making art. My enormous needs for sex and conversation tapped him dry, and he wasn't inspired. He still hadn't manifested the funds to fix the van. The As If Principle wasn't working because he didn't have the space to focus. "But I got rid of my cat," I whined, frightened and wimpy and clingy. One morning I got up early and fixed him Eggs Benedict. He took one bite and snarled, "This hollandaise is awful." Around this same time, Ned's mother, Fran, invited me to a NOW meeting for a slide lecture by feminist cartoonist Nicole Hollander. "Nicole Hollander," I practically shrieked with excitement. "I love her *Feminist Funnies!*" Nicole Hollander's presentation was both hysterical and inspirational, and sharing that womyn's space with Fran, I couldn't believe how lucky I was to have her as my future mother-in law. After the lecture, we sloshed down frozen daiquiris at the Palmer House. With her dark hair, large jewelry and adored cat, Miaou, she reminded me of Sylvia from Hollander's comic strip. She clinked her glass against mine. "To you, my darling," she said. "Hemingway invented this drink." "Really!" I said. "Yes, really." We talked for hours, Fran arcing the air with her arms or shaking her fist at the ceiling, mesmerizing me with memories of McCarthy-era phone taps and the heartbreak of Chairman Mao. I'd never before met an older woman I could look up to, could rap with. I told her my dreams, my insecurities. "Such beautiful hair you have," she said. "When we were at the pool your strawberry hair looked so lovely against the black of your suit. I wish I looked half as good as you in a bathing suit." I told her about my poetry. "You're so smart and strong, you can do anything you put your mind to." When I told her how few women authors I'd read in my undergrad comp lit classes, and how I'd been reading nothing but women since then in order to catch up, Fran invited me to her book club. "We're reading *Women on the Edge of Time*." "I love that book. I saw Marge Piercy when she came to IU, and she said she had an abortion so no baby would interfere with her writing. She said a woman writer has to make tough choices." "You would have made a great communist," Fran said. She set down her frozen daiquiri and leaned in closer, enveloping me in Chanel No. 5. "I wish my daughter was like you, instead of buried away in the woods. What sane woman lives in a tower in the woods." Ned's sister was a forest ranger, an occupation she pursued, according to Ned, in order to stay as far away as possible from Fran. "I'm worried Ned's growing tired of me," I blurted. "You are so much better for him than that white trash gold digger, Neva. Don't sell yourself short." The waiter deposited another round of daiquiris on our table, and she continued. "Ned's an idiot. Such a disappointment." She took a gulp of rummy slush, shook her head. "He was a promising boy, but look at him, he lives in a fantasy. Don't believe anything he says." When I returned, Ned whiffed the alcohol on my breath and withdrew. "I don't want to be around your lower vibrations. Stay away from my mother. She's poison."

The more things crumbled between Ned and me, the closer I became to Fran. She was unrelentingly critical of him, which at the time delighted me, that his own mother would take my side—but now I wonder if having the type of mother who would side against him with a woman she'd just met doesn't explain some of Ned's narcissistic dreaminess. Before Fran's glaring critical eye, who wouldn't find strategies to tune out. He'd launch into one excited rant after another about his plans to promote his art, to start a business, write a book, sell herbal tonics—it was like he was throwing his whole being into an idea—but there was never any follow-through, just more plans. He'd open his mouth with zeal in his eyes, and I'd cringe at the prospect of having to act enthused. Outside the bubble of college students who comprised the Bloomington chapter, I was to meet many cultists who lacked a reality principle—the cult was flypaper to such people—but Ned was my first. He was a higher initiate— he was supposed to be special, he was supposed to guide me. I'd imagined us cross-legged on his living room floor, eyes closed, bodies left behind as we soared across the universe, sharing new worlds. Meditating for half an hour a day was a big deal in the cult, but he rarely did it. I didn't believe he'd ever traveled to a higher plane, that

he'd ever attained any sort of realization. I should have dropped out
of the cult right then, for after Ned, the energy it took to suppress
my bullshit meter was enormous. Several years later I met his new
girlfriend, a cultist who—I'm not making this up—also claimed to
be from Jupiter. It was winter and we were standing behind a car
and there was snow in the street. Ned was there too, but several feet
away, talking to somebody else. The girlfriend was incredibly normal
looking, with long straight brown hair, doe eyes, and navy peacoat.
A bit younger than I. She cocked her head and asked softly, "Why
does Ned lie?" She seemed so confused and innocent, hands stuffed
into woolen pockets.

I didn't know what to do—I'd given up my apartment for this
cramped cottage with a stranger who was both rejecting and boring
me. I had to leave, but I had no money, nowhere to go. I subsisted
on coarse dark rye bread with cheddar cheese and alfalfa sprouts,
and I walked for hours in Lincoln Park, trying to shake off the waves
of anxiety that coursed through me. Finally, one night, Ned yelled,
"I can't take this any more. Get out." And he didn't mean the next
morning, he meant right then. It was dark out. So I found myself
bawling into the intercom of a woman I knew from work, "Can I
stay here tonight." I sold all my stuff, bought a plane ticket to San
Francisco, crashed on friends' couches for six weeks (including a few
tense nights with Bob and Susie), and saved up as much money as I
could from freelance graphics jobs. I felt terrified and desperate and
hopelessly unlovable. Until I met Dietmar.

Dietmar was blond, fine boned, cherubic. I'd seen him at various cult activities, and we'd engaged in casual chitchat, the way all the local cultists did. It was like we were ducks in the same litter; warmth was a given. Then one afternoon he asked me out for coffee to "discuss a business matter." Dietmar had written a success module that he planned to sell through direct marketing by taking out ads in the backs of magazines. He wanted me to design his logo. I freelanced as a board artist for corporate slide shows, which means I did a lot of cutting and pasting and inking straight lines. I made maps and bar charts and speaker support slides. I pasted the names of a thousand Avon ladies on animation cells, each name in the same position so they could double-expose the Avon lady's name beneath her smiling portrait. I made slides for McDonalds that read "Wait Two Minutes" and "Turn Patties Now." I knew little about graphic design or producing material for print, but Dietmar was cute so I said yes. Though he was only 24, Dietmar had been working at a technology giant for several years. He was proud to be the youngest person (nineteen at the time) the corporation had ever hired, and so he wrote a manual that shared his secrets to success, step by step. The logo I came up with was a series of alternating black and white squares inside one another—like a bullseye, but square; like the cult's logo, but square. I made the original really big then shrunk it down on the stat machine, to minimize my wobbles. Dietmar loved it.

Night after night we sat in diners talking, walked through Lincoln Park talking, drove along the lake talking until our throats were hoarse and morning beckoned. Dietmar wasn't a higher initiate, and I found that so soothing, so permissive. I shared my dreams of being a writer, and he shared his secrets to success—*lists, affirmations, etc.* He had that Rasputin gleam of a true believer, and I absorbed it all uncritically: his words, his compact body, mischievous smile. I told him about Nance and my failed semester as a photography student at the Institute of Design, how in Bloomington I somehow ended up with a book by the first Western Master and used to read it when I was stoned until it all started to make sense, how I went to an introductory lecture and joined the cult and stopped doing drugs, how all the gay guys from college moved to San Francisco and I was planning to join them. When I eventually got around to Ned—*He threw me out in the middle of the night!* sniffle sniffle—Dietmar looked wonderfully livid. "Ned's a jerk," he said, leaning closer and running his fingers through my hair, gently, like he was petting a kitten. "Neva went through the same shit with him." And then he told me that he ghostwrote *Jovial I Am.* I was stunned, but that was just the beginning—Dietmar had had an affair with Neva! Something that Ned was totally unaware of. It all started on a cross-country car trip the three of them took to a national cult conference on the west coast and then to the Nevada desert to meet Neva's uncle's flying saucer. Ned and Neva in the front seat, Dietmar in the back—as Ned drove, Neva kept catching Dietmar's eye in the rearview mirror, flirting with him. This went on for days. He was a mere boy—she was wild and multi-worldly—and the sparks were flying. He said she fucked like a wild cat. He said Ned tormented Neva with his commitment issues. It was only after she and Dietmar wrote the book and Ned thought there was money to be made that he finally married her.

I asked Dietmar if he believed Neva's story. He said she was very convincing, her memories of Jupiter were so detailed; and she was beyond eccentric, with this power over people—and animals—like one time when they were sailing on the lake, out of nowhere comes this big butterfly, "a monarch with the orange, a beautiful butterfly. You think, in the middle of Lake Michigan, where's this butterfly coming from." It fluttered and landed on Neva's shoulder and stayed there for hours. Wherever she went, butterflies would appear as if she'd summoned them; she'd hold out her hand and they'd quiver over and sit on it. In all the hours Dietmar spent talking with her about Jupiter, Neva never once contradicted herself. I keep replaying the scene of the three of them in the dead of night driving through the desert to meet Uncle Nandaz's flying saucer ... around them are vast stars and moonbeams casting cactus shadows ... all is silent save the whirring crunch of wheels on the dusty two-lane road, the occasional screech of coyote or bird. It drives me crazy that I don't know what happens when they arrive. I squeeze my mind but no new details arise—I even email Dietmar and ask him, but he doesn't answer. I'm sure he didn't see a saucer, *that* I would remember. This is a novel, so you'd think I could just improvise an ending—but Neva's actual behavior is consistently more rousing than anything I could come up with. I am an imaginative lightweight compared to her. Maybe the spaceship was vibrating on a higher plane and that's why they couldn't see it.

We cruise along Lake Shore Drive on a perfectly fresh summer evening; the lights the water the curves in the road seem hyper-real because I'm leaving for San Francisco in a week, and we're in love. Dietmar plays "California Girls" on the 8-track over and over, and says he's sure that people will drive me up and down the coast of California just to spend time with me. He tells me he's so sure I'll accomplish great things, he's going to keep a file on me and track my progress. After three weeks of talking I'm going to die if we don't have sex. Dietmar was resistant at first but now he wants to go for it—but he lives with his German immigrant mother and I don't live anywhere. That night we fucked in his car, and later that week on a friend's couch—then a secretary from work let me crash at her father's condo while he was away at a work retreat—he was an executive at the corporate office of Montgomery Ward, and his girlfriend was a hippie from San Francisco. I had lunch with them once. The girlfriend served us sangria and a platter of caviar, chopped eggs, and marinated spaghetti squash. She said I'd love San Francisco, that I could get food stamps and general assistance—free food was everywhere and there was free music in the park, and if I got pregnant the state would pay for the abortion. You didn't need any money to live in San Francisco. When I moved there I found all these things to be true. The Ward executive was recently divorced, and he didn't have much. A leather La-Z-Boy recliner stood in the center of the otherwise empty living room. Waiting for Dietmar to come over, I stretched out on it, surrounded by an expanse of bare wooden floor, sipping icy mineral water from an oversized wine glass, listening to *Music for Airports,* watching the breeze play with the sheer white curtains, a sparse luxury that made my heart flutter. The next thing I remember is fucking in the bed and the Ward executive walking in on us. My final night in Chicago, Dietmar treated us to a hotel room. We'd fuck and fuck and fuck, pull apart and collapse on our backs, panting and spouting gooey love drool, then fuck fuck fuck. Dietmar spoke German while we did it, which I thought was so hot, and then he said talk dirty to me, and I said fuck my pussy you fucker and he slammed against me with a frenzy. We fucked on the bed until we slid with the quilted floral bedspread onto the floor, where we fucked until we got rug burns, then we fucked and splashed in the bathtub then back on the bed; we fucked for six hours straight, luxuriating in being alone together. We were not bigger than life, we were not higher initiates or incarnated beings from a more advanced planet—we were little people having ordinary Earthling sex. I could feel his energy glinting in every chakra, it was glorious. The next morning he drove me to the airport and I bawled my head off.

In 1977 an undergrad at Cal State Northridge accused the first Western Master of plagiarism. While working on a term paper, the student stumbled upon passages from books self-published by another cult inserted in our cult's bible and other sacred teachings that were supposedly dictated by the Ascended Masters, including *The Secret Gospels of Primeval Prophecy*. The deeper the student dug, the more lifted passages he found until it became clear that the bulk of our cult's books were lifted from other sources—and it wasn't from just that one marginal cult—the first Western Master harvested text from all over the place, including the best-selling *Way of the Sufi* by Indries Shah. The injunction our cult filed against the student failed, and a paperback edition of his 120-page religious studies term paper sold out in three weeks. I didn't hear about the scandal until 1980. I was living on Folsom Street in San Francisco, sitting on my frameless double mattress, my back leaning against the wall—cultists remember where they were when they heard about the plagiarism the way people remember where they were when Kennedy was shot or the Twin Towers collapsed or when the big quake of 1989 struck—I was on the phone with Dietmar. He ranted on and on about how the teachings were a lie, that we'd been duped, his voice quivering with betrayal. My shock quickly turned to rage—the arrow of my bullshit meter that Ned had pushed into the red was now racing around in circles, shooting off sparks. You'd think I would have terminated my membership the next day—but no—that took another couple of years. Cults are sticky as chewed gum. A few months later I received a letter from Dietmar—it was more of a note, written in ballpoint on lined notebook paper. He said the Masters were real, he knew this from experience, and he was now a higher initiate and in charge of half of Texas. No explanation for his dramatic turnaround, no I'm sorry for destroying your faith. "Fuck you," I said as I tore up his letter. That was the end of him in my life—good riddance—until social networking was developed and I found him on Linked In. I messaged him and he wrote back, "So what have you been doing the past 30 years?" A question so big it I sputtered and gasped. Here I am, 30 years later, still trying to figure out if there's anything I can believe, if there's any system to this chaos other than DNA and the ultimate erosion of all of us, wondering why there's still a place in my heart for this guy I only knew for a month, my 24-year-old nymph whispering to me in German, making the incomprehensible so sexy. In the cult I loved people in a way I've not experienced since. It's hard to love people in the *let me see your CV before I decide whether or not to talk to you* arts world. In the cult I was nobody and the people I loved were nobodies—these were people I could trust— and they could trust me—my love I gave freely, and it was received gladly. Through the lens of Soul, everyone was beautiful—even Bob, impossible Bob. The lives of people outside the cult seemed so harsh—I often wondered how they managed without this matrix of love that caressed me, airy and sweet as cotton candy.

It was taboo to talk of the scandal, but we all did. Even we who didn't read the book found our faith shaken. Thousands left the path. In the cult's monthly newsletter, the current Master wrote that plagiarism is a limited point of view. He reminded us of the temples of learning on the Etheric Plane, wherein is stored all knowledge. Creative geniuses—such as the first Western Master—bring back wisdom from these temples to the physical world. This is why two people in different parts of the globe can simultaneously come up with the same idea, why our cult's texts are so similar to those of others. Our sacred terms are not corruptions of Hindu words, he continued. Quite the opposite—Hinduism borrowed these words from our cult. The Master warned that should we ever leave the path, we'd lose all our initiations, our spiritual growth would stop, and we'd be at the mercy of the dark forces. But I did leave. After ten years of filtering every thought, every action through the cult's teaching, I dropped out. As someone wrote on a cult survivors site, "I felt as if someone had just torn out my insides and served them to me over rice." Without the cult, my interior spaces are vast and lonely, a tornado-flattened terrain. I stumble around in a daze— no markers, no roads, no trees or shrubs or telephone poles, no verticality whatsoever, just these melting corpses of field mice and snakes. Ravaged gray land meets gray sky along a horizon so faint it all but disappears. My throat opens and I cry out, "Master, oh, Master!" I can't bear to live without him. Love spills from my mouth for him, love spills from my ears for him, love belches from my heart for him, love seeps from my nipples and cunt and armpits for him, slickly red love flows from my nose, spills over my lower lip and down my chin. Master, I don't care what you did come back please please please. Come. Back. When your world falls apart, pain opens to a marvel so tender, beautiful and ugly merge. Meaning is beaten away like dust from an exquisitely imperfect Persian rug. You see colors. Lines of inky swirls. But no meaning. It took years to recover. I'm not sure I did recover.

In 1995, I write a cover story for a free weekly about the cult. They fly me to San Diego to attend a Saturday afternoon presentation by my excommunicated Master. I go with Blaine, the student who exposed the plagiarism, who has since become a professional cultbuster. The program is called "The Universal Basics of Life Through Music." It costs $35 at the door. At the Hawaiian-themed hotel, I take my seat among the forty or so other seekers, many of them former cultists who have flown in for the event. Beside me, Blaine looks boyish, in forest green shorts, tan canvas shirt, white Velcro-fastened running shoes, crew socks, and shag hair cut. I've attempted a more professional effect—black linen skirt, muted teal silk jacket and black ankle boots. I look like a temp, like a very good temp. A young perky assistant, Dawn, is finishing an applied kinesiology demonstration of the power of the Master's music. A volunteer raises his arm straight out to the side, and Dawn easily pushes it down. Then she asks him to think about the Master's music as he again holds out his arm. This time the arm doesn't budge no matter how hard she pushes down on it. "See!" she exclaims. We close our eyes and chant together for several minutes. The Master enters and takes his position behind the gold-toned vibes. Remembering him in his better days, thin and attractive, I am shocked by the corpulent aging man standing before me, coughing. He reminds me of the bloated near-death Elvis, only fatter and older. He jokes about his "Nevada cold," blaming it on the dust from the Indian burial grounds being dug up to build housing. His movements are frail and slow as he removes his dark blue jacket to reveal a short-sleeved white shirt and tan pants held up with wide red suspenders. Accompanied by a devotee keyboardist, the Master begins with "Blues in E Flat." The music is great, lethargic and soothing, the kind of music one should listen to in a cocktail lounge with an umbrellaed drink. The Master smiles to himself as he hits the vibes. He seems gently ecstatic, but so tired. When he finishes the song, he takes off his shoes "to be closer to the keys." The atmosphere in the room is homey and protective. After a couple more tunes, the Master is joined by a vocalist, an attractive woman with carefully mussed dark hair. In a deep, velvety voice she sings, "Don't blame me for falling in love with you. I'm under your spell, but how can I help it." There is a double edge to this torch song—from the way she keeps glancing affectionately over at the Master, it is the Master's spell that she can't be blamed for falling under. When she begins her next selection, "My Funny Valentine," I lose all objectivity. Valentine's Day, my birthday, is only three days away, and I feel nostalgic for the boyfriends who played this song for me. The loss of my old loves and my Master's loss of status become merged in an ineffable sadness. Even more moving is her rendition of "Somewhere Over the Rainbow." My Master sits this one out on a rattan stool, his arms folded over his huge stomach, lost in thought. When the vocalist gets to the line about the chimney tops, I focus on my Master's bulbous belly and red suspenders. He looks like Santa, like a fallen Santa. Even though Blaine's been cultbusting this man for eighteen years, he has tears in his eyes. I lean against his arm and whisper, "You are so opaque." Sitting in this pathetic room with its riotously floral turquoise and purple carpet, it feels as if nobody's dreams will ever come true. We zone out on lounge music for an hour and a half, then the Master walks to the front of the room and says, "That's it." I ask Blaine if he's going to introduce himself. Blaine shakes his head. "I don't want to tweak his day. He's got his music. He's having a good time." So I go over by myself and shake his hand. "I used to be in the cult," I tell him. Discomfort spreads across his face as I continue, "You were my Master most of the time I was in it." Holding my hand he looks deep into my eyes and says, "I'm still your Master. I always have been. I never stopped, not even for a minute—even though they, pardon my expression, treated me like shit." As I walk away he yells after me, "Hang in there!"

When my article was reposted online, I started receiving emails from men who claimed to have been attacked by demons sent by the Master. *I was given the initiation in a short ceremony during the afternoon. In the evening, as soon as I sat down to contemplate, I was attacked by a swarm of demons. They appeared around my "third eye" as a group of 10-20 little fiery lights, rather like a swarm of angry bees. They continually lunged against my forehead, trying to gain entry. ... I sensed someone swimming near me. I did not see them, but evaded them. A demonic creature appeared in front of me. It was a giant demon, out of a Hieronymus Bosch painting. ... We never think to ask how the Masters differ from demons. As I found out through hard experience, they don't! They are fallen angels disguising themselves as angels of light.* These messages so alarmed and depressed me, I begged the site to remove my email address. We opened ourselves to the Master, we opened ourselves to the light—we opened and opened and opened until we became porous sponges sucking up energy. After I left the cult, I would hook into the emotional essence of a person and not be able to shut it off. Walking past a schizophrenic shouting into a dumpster would fry me. Riding public transportation was a nightmare, in every direction all these beings with their intense feelings zapping through me. Panic. Whenever I left the house I felt panic. Except for an occasional twinge, the panic has left but I can still feel weird energy a block away—from that distance I may not be able to make out what a person looks like, but I can sense what's going on, the way my cat Ted knows I'm planning on taking him to the vet, no matter how hard I try to hide it. If that weird-energy person happened to be in the same room as me, any room, public or private, I couldn't concentrate. If I had a regular job where I had to sit in an office with someone else for eight hours a day, even if my coworker didn't say a word to me, it would utterly exhaust me. I don't just love, I absorb people, and everybody suffers. This is why I've become so rigid.

From a cult survivors site: *I could only find info on a Dodie Bellamy who wrote about Horror, all aspects of sexuality, and who is married to a gay man. Is this the same one who did the write up on the cult and the excommunicated Master? I have to admit that I am very conventional in many aspects of my life, so I was rather shocked to discover that this Dodie Bellamy wrote such graphic material as I found under her name.*

In 1991, at a UFO convention in Tucson, Arizona, Neva reemerged as Nikwuz Nerpuz. Nikwuz made quite a splash. "Maybe it was the Chicago accent combined with blood-red nail polish, combined with spiked silver heels—which collectively upstaged her alien intelligence, like the floating vixen in a magic show. Everyone wanted to interrogate her. Video crews lined up like 747s circling the airport." The next sighting of Neva is in Germany, where the translation of her book, *Jovial Ich Bin,* is a big seller. She's all over YouTube—in ice blonde helmet hair and white dress, Neva explains to a German audience that the Earth was populated by visitors from many planets, many races. In outer space the races do not mingle, for each race has its own planet. Neva's race, the artistic, refined

Aryan race, originated on Jupiter. She uses the term Aryan as if it were a neutral, as if she and her German fans were unaware of the violent histories that cling to it. All races are equal, she adds, for all beings are of Soul. In every image I find—and there are dozens—she's wearing white—white sleeveless shift as she twirls in a field of wildflowers, exquisitely cut white skirt suit, white silk Chinese jacket, pearl earrings, ivory leotard and ballet slippers as she demonstrates a dramatic dip during a Jovian dance workshop.

On the Galactic Channel's Spiritual Forum, "Ashtar" has posted a video of her 1993 appearance on the Jerry Springer show. I sit in my suitably space-aged gray mesh desk chair and watch all 43 minutes of it. The camera cuts from Jerry to a petite woman in a white wide-skirted dress with a plunging scalloped neckline. Her hair is a platinum bowl cut, her fingernails elongated opaline ovals. When Jerry addresses her as Neva, she raises her perky upturned nose and says, "Please call me Nikwuz."

Jerry's hands fly though the air like unmanned shuttles. He bounces.

Jerry: You'll excuse the skepticism, but we don't meet people from Jupiter everyday.

Nikwuz: I existed on a different dimension than what you understand on Earth.

Neva's Jovian manner is neutral bordering on stern, her mouth a flat horizon.

Jerry: How old would you be if you were on Jupiter?

Nikwuz: I would be 250.

Jerry's eyes and mouth gape open as he stumbles backwards in surprise.

Jerry: You look great.

Nikwuz: Thank you.

Jerry: I'm willing to believe. I'm not here to make fun.

Nikwuz: I was raised on the Astral Plane on Ganymede, the largest moon of Jupiter. In the Jovian Temple of History I learned that Earth, the youngest of the planets in this solar system, is plagued by the imbalance caused by its singular moon. It was hard for me to adjust to life on Earth, all the violence and different races.

Her mouth opens wide with her careful enunciation. Her head swivels slowly from left to right, chin tilting slightly for emphasis.

Jerry: Have you ever, uh, been intimate with an Earthling?

Nikwuz: I was married.

Jerry: Married, really. To an Earthling!

Nikwuz: Yes. He's in the audience.

Ned stands up, and Jerry rushes to him with a microphone. In his suit jacket, open collared white shirt, and bright cornflower blue scarf, Ned's thicker but still handsome enough to turn a girl's head.

Jerry: What a loving, gracious wife you have.

Ned: Ex-wife.

Jerry wobbles his head and shakes his shoulders.

Jerry: Ex-wife! I walked right into that. Sorry. Did her story have anything to do with your breaking up?

Ned: Not really. Neva told me her story the night that we met and I always had a sense of destiny about our being together. I supported her while she was writing the book. I've always been a very open-minded person so it was not difficult for me to not only believe, but to know it was true and that it was in fact my destiny to help her, to support her to get the word out.

Head bent to meet Jerry's mic, Ned stands stone still and dignified, but his left hand dances nonstop, up and down, over and back, swooping and spinning through the air. The hand is so active it seems to be broadcasting a secret code to the audience, to me. I think of poker and I wonder if the hand is Ned's tell. As Ned smiles, laughs, turns serious, the hand points, flips, shakes, cups and bounces up and down as if it were tossing an invisible ball.

Jerry: This would be the greatest story in the history of the world, it really would, because it would refute everything we've learned—if this were the greatest story ever told, why is it always out on some farm out in some place where they land that nobody ever hears of. That's the skepticism. It's a pretty big story, and she's just here on the talk show. Which is great, but wouldn't it be more than that?

Jerry crouches and touches the ground for emphasis.

Ned: People often laugh, and she hasn't been taken seriously. But the way the planet is so rapidly changing, the consciousness has evolved to the point now where people are beginning to accept the possibility that this is in fact real.

Ned pushes his palm toward the viewer. His hand is saying—Dodie, how could you write such shit about me. The hand is saying—for bedding the dark forces you've earned yourself six more lifetimes of heavy karma. The hand is saying—meet me on the inner with your sweet pussy.

Jerry: So you thoroughly believe her.

Ned: I know it's true.

The camera tightens in on Ned's shoulders and head, but occasionally the hand's fingers leap up from the bottom of the frame.

Jerry: Good, good for you.

Jerry brings on an astronomer to test Neva's claim that a city named Anahatar exists on Ganymede on the Physical Plane. Anahatar is where Neva manifested a physical body before she came to Earth in a space ship.

Scientist: The daytime temperatures on Ganymede are 171 to 297 degrees below zero. How could you survive temperatures that low?

Nikwuz: The city's under a climactic dome.

Scientist: Is this a big city?

Nikwuz: Not terribly big, but not small.

Neva is unearthly still. Her mouth and eyes are the only parts that move, like the frozen faces of overbotoxed women.

Scientist: Is it bigger than a football field.

Nikwuz: Yes, it's bigger than that.

Scientist: We've mapped the surface of Ganymede, we've mapped everything the size of a football field or larger. We've never seen any city.

Nikwuz: It's covered by clouds and gasses.

Scientist: Our instruments see through clouds and gasses.

Neva lifts her nose in the air and gives the slightest hint of an eyeroll.

Her hands clench the armrests of her chair. The chair looks too large for her.

Nikwuz: Scientists think they know everything. Keep looking.

Scientist: Could you give me the coordinates of your city? Then I could better find it.

Neva's eyes blink rapidly. She looks down, takes a breath, and responds without emotion. Each movement of her head so subtle, it's hypnotic.

Nikwuz: I'd have to give you my address and phone number to contact me later for that information. I'd have to ask my uncle, the scientist in my family, who travels around on a spaceship.

Jerry gesticulates wildly, cringes, pulls the mic in close, hunches, throws his arms above his head, rhythmically beats his hand in the air, back and forth, like a metronome.

Jerry: With my whole heart I want to believe you. The audience wants to believe you. All we want is a little proof.

Nikwuz: I know.

Jerry bends over, squats, purses his lips, puts a finger to his mouth. He never stops moving. Children must love him, he's so grand, and flexible. If you ran full speed into Jerry he'd bend backwards and you'd pass right over him and crash into the wall. Neva would stop you before you got near her, invisible rays beaming from her eyes. You'd stand there frozen in mid-motion while she looked on, implacable and a bit bored. Ned is so solid I could come running toward him from across the auditorium and with the force of my momentum hurl myself into his body, and he wouldn't flinch. As I bounced off of him broken and bloodied, he'd continue: "The consciousness of mankind has reached . . ." As if I didn't exist.

The video is a big hit on the Galactic Channel site. *Thanks for posting this cool video, Ashtar :) I'd just watched it when I saw a very bright star out the window.* Nikwuz seems sincere! *I've seen a lot of interviews with her, I think she's definitely for real.* I do believe she is telling the truth. *Always liked Nikwuz. There's a great presence about her. But man how lucky do you have to be to score with a Jovian chick. On their first date she's like: oh I'm from Jupiter and we're gonna have kids, and he's like: ok no problem let's get started.* There was 1 key statement Nikwuz said that proved she was from Jupiter and has the DNA. *Call me nuts, but I really like this lady. If she is nuts she makes a pretty convincing alien.* She has such a wise and loving look in her eyes. *Nikwuz looks really uncomfortable in the video because she is telepathic; she can read those people's (audience) thoughts; so she talks real fast, overwhelmed by their energy and negative thinking. Bless her!* I love her composure. I know it isn't easy, the work she has done and is doing. *She appears to be genuine to me—and what unemotional presence she has, in the face of all that ridicule.*

On Ganymede, Nikwuz chanted a special mantra to lower her vibrations to the point where she could enter Anahatar, the one city on Ganymede that exists on the Physical Plane. There she manifested a material body and traveled by rocket ship to Khachöpelri, a monastery hidden in the mountains of Northern Tibet. When he was a boy, Jesus Christ studied in the same monastery. It has hard for Nikwuz to adjust to a physical body. "I felt like I was in a suit of armor, limited in movements and what I could see and observe." She did not know how to sleep, go to the bathroom, eat, or use her vocal cords. When she refused to poop, the Tibetan monks laughed and told her, "You have to do this to live in the Physical." And so she did. But she didn't like it. Each day the monks would laugh at some new thing that Nikwuz refused to do. To this day she eats very little, for food is alien to her refined Jovian system. Eventually she adjusted to gravity and learned to speak English. Then she traveled to Tennessee to help the Earth child Neva through her birth process. There she received the genetic imprint of Neva's physical body, so that when Neva died in the bus crash and Nikwuz replaced her, no one noticed the difference. But there were differences. Nikwuz manufactures her own calcium and she's on her second set of teeth. Her extraordinarily high blood pressure is necessary for her to maintain a physical embodiment. If Nikwuz's blood pressure were as low as an earthling's, she'd be in a coma. Nikwuz's high vibratory energy speeds up the karma of those around her. "Fear is the biggest tool for control in your societies," she says, carefully articulating "so-ci-e-ties" with equal emphasis on each syllable.

I recently met a woman who used to be in the inner circle of Amma, the hugging saint. For the privilege of following Amma around the world, working for her, she paid Amma a monthly stipend. She also paid for her own accommodations and travel. The student now lives in Sea Ranch, a swanky planned community in Mendocino, with a private redwood forest and beach. Each morning she does freeform dances along the ocean in the coves you need a permit to enter. As we sit around her kitchen table drinking tea, the student says Amma controlled all aspects of their lives. If you were in a relationship, you couldn't have sex or break up without Amma's permission. I ask her if Amma had any scandals. She said yes, Amma's handmaiden quit because Amma—whose unconditional love is so vast she can hug a football stadium's worth of people, one by one—was so mean to her. "That's it?" I say. "It caused a huge uproar in the community. Many senior students left." Whenever I come across a spiritual teacher, I google their name + "scandal," and then I sit back and enjoy the fireworks. After five years of guru guy after guy stealing money and fucking with a frenzy—how does this woman guru misbehave? She's mean to a handmaiden! I feel the claustrophobia of female roles closing in on me—high-collared rigidity—libidinal squelching—an ever watchful eye—obsession with minutiae—tedium—nuns with shaven heads mincing about, unwanted women with nowhere else to go—my mother caring how well her neighbor washes her floor. Before all this, Neva's libidinal excess is thrilling. In my survey of pants-dropping drunken spiritual shysters, Neva is the female heart, as vivid and outlandish as the best of them, a white-headed Jean Harlow who descends from the heavens in all her radiant Aryan glory. I can't quit stalking her online, relishing each tender detail. Her heart beats faster than our hearts; she heals faster, ages slower. She loves all living beings—animal, mineral and human. She preaches that reality is whatever you believe, that the U.S. government is allowing bad aliens to abduct its citizens in exchange for alien technology, that dinosaurs are intelligent aliens who mutated because of radiation and lost their intelligence. Her look hardens over time, cigarette hanging from the corner of blood red lips. If I stare long enough, I hope I will somehow penetrate her, or better yet, her gaze will penetrate me, who slept with two of her former partners. Nikwuz Nerpuz. She and her Uncle Nandaz are from an ancient Jovian family. Their names begin with N because N has a specific energy. The Z at the end is an honorific. It's not really translatable into English, but a close approximation would be Beneficent Colonizing Teacher. The energetic vibrations of N and Z allow Jovian visitors to stay tuned into Earth consciousness. Nikwuz turns her platinum head, elegant as an insect. "Karma stopped in 1999 for all mankind," she declares, and I imagine I've absorbed some of her aura, in the spray of those two cocks that had been *inside* her. I do not feel such desire for images of Ned. Of me, he writes on his blog: *I always loved her. She taught me to put miso in soup.*

As I search through an old journal, an insert falls out. I unfold the legal-sized sheet to reveal a sketch of a naked woman holding a nail file. The paper has yellowed, the ink faded. The artist has used a spare, unshaded line, purposely naive, like a Matisse. The woman is many months pregnant, a single curved line for each eye, another curve for belly button. Circles designate the large areolas of pointy, pendulous breasts. Her arms are raised, covering the tips of the breasts, just a hint of right nipple. Her hands are too small for her arms, the fingers cramped curly cues. There aren't enough of them. The overall impression is one of peace and intimacy. On the bottom right is written "Neva does her nails 3/2/71 NAN." I do a double take. This can't be my Neva, this can't be by my Ned, drawn seven years before I met him. Neva looks unselfconscious, comfortable as a cow. Of course she does her nails naked. There is no contradiction between her unguarded exposure and her labor at manicuring a persona. Perhaps this is the secret behind all successful charismatics, the way they create a unified field around traits that in others would be confusing. The Master unrepentantly fucks a zillion students, drinks himself to death, and is a great spiritual teacher. To his followers, he isn't great *despite* the other traits. Rather, the whole enchilada *is* his greatness, and it is their mandate to transcend any limited mindsets that would have a problem with this. The paradox of the Master is a lesson, a gift. Neva never apologizes for behavior that challenges conventional notions of spirituality. The truly free, she says repeatedly, are not hampered by Earth moralities and expectations, which were created by the U.S. government to control us.

During meditation practice, the Teacher stoops down and touches the student's back, gently correcting her alignment. The heat from his hand sends a charge down her spine, magenta, which spirals back up vermillion. She can feel the blood racing through her veins, its sinuous percussion. *I am alive,* she thinks, *truly alive.* The next day she drops by during the Teacher's office hours. She stands in his doorway, in her knee-skimming white linen skirt and white tank top cut low enough to reveal a hint, just a hint, of her white lace bra, and blurts out, "I have a question about meditation." The Teacher smiles gently. "I was expecting you. Would you like some rooibos? I just heated some water." They sit on either side of his large wooden desk, sipping their tea and talking about movies. The Teacher has just seen the French *Lady Chatterley's Lover.* "There's this scene where the lovers frolic naked in the rain; their innocence is beautiful," he says. "We don't see enough images of the innocence of love." He catches her eye. Tiny beads of sweat line his upper lip. The conversation turns to Giorgio Agamben. The Teacher says, "Agamben argues that in the capitalist cult everything is profaned." "I never thought of it that way," she replies, "but, wow, yes." The Teacher remains silent, a knowing smile on his full lips. *Agamben,* she thinks, *say something else about Agamben,* but before the Teacher's gaze—she's never met anyone so profound, so intense—she can't recall a single thing Agamben has written. Then, oh yeah—his talk in Berkeley! "I once went to this lecture that Agamben gave, and you know how he has that really thick accent?" The Teacher nods. "Where was this?" "At UC Berkeley, in Wheeler Hall. It was a couple years ago, and he was talking about structures outside the juridical system, you know, like duty-free shops in airports, and he kept bringing up 'bird life,' and I got all excited and wrote 'bird life' in my journal. Then afterwards when I went out for drinks with a friend, she said he wasn't saying 'bird life,' he was saying 'birth life.' I felt like such a goof!" The Teacher throws his head back and emits a belly laugh, his white teeth glistening. She takes in the simplicity of his office—behind him a wall of windows overlooks the lotus garden. To his right a dorm-sized refrigerator and a small table holding tea paraphernalia and a brass singing bowl, above it the familiar red and gold silk wall hanging embroidered with the eight auspicious symbols: lotus, conch shell, endless knot, treasure vase, parasol, golden fish, dharma wheel, victory banner—she could recite them in her sleep. The Teacher clears his throat. He has stopped laughing and is drinking her in with his eyes, his intense hazel eyes which see into the truth of who she really is. Such nakedness terrifies her, and she breaks his gaze, scans the wall of books to his left—spiritual texts both contemporary and ancient—East Indian, African, Chinese, Native American, populist New Age—also philosophy, anthropology, Jungian psychology, poetry. "You read poetry!" she exclaims. "Yes, I've loved it since I was a teen." He takes down *The Collected Poems of Jack Spicer* and reads, "Breaking a branch of impossible/ Green-stemmed hyacinth/ You have found thorns and postulated a rose./ Sometimes we were almost like lovers/ (As the sun almost touches the earth at sunset)/ But,/ At touch,/ The horse leapt like an ox/ Into another orbit of roses, roses." He holds her gaze. "This poem reminds me of you. 'Another orbit of roses.'" The student's heart is racing. "I can see something inside you that no one else can," he says. The Teacher looks down at his wristwatch, his cinnamon-colored forearm luscious against his white polo shirt, alligator logo over his heart like a pledge. "I have another appointment—but I so enjoy talking with you," he says, rising from his chair. "Come visit me again. Please." She glances at the wall hanging—the tirelessly cheery red and gold of it—*lotus conch shell parasol victory banner*—and boldly meets the Teacher's sultry amber eyes. Their gazes lock, and she says, "How about tomorrow?"

In another video, Neva arrives three hours late for her German going away party, which is held in the parlor of the small castle in which she lives. To the obviously upset guests she says, "Just because the party started at three o'clock doesn't mean I would be there at three. We should have made that clearer on the invitation. Party begins at three o'clock, Nikwuz arrives at six." Neva has deftly shifted the room's reality to her reality—three hours late is no longer late, it is on time. She says she was so frazzled with people knocking on her door, asking her if she was ready, she didn't have time to do her nails. In the degraded quality of YouTube her fingers look perfectly polished, pearlescent white. I pick up other bits of her party chitchat. She's doing fine, the doctors say the high blood pressure is genetic, they say it's better to have high blood pressure and good kidneys. There's something about her having to leave Germany—she was crying, they threatened to put her in jail. She's wearing a sheer white cape embossed with silver stars and moons. Beneath it is a backless white tank that plunges in the front. "I tried to put on a bra," she says, "but it wouldn't stick, so I'm not wearing one. I'm indecent. But I wanted to wear my Jovian outfit." She lets the back of her cape slip to show off a bright butterfly tattoo on her right shoulder blade. The sides of her pants are slit. All the way up. When she sits smoking a Marlboro Menthol, she crosses her legs, and the pants fall away, revealing the tops of her thighs. Even though she's nearly sixty in Earth years, she has trim, shapely legs. Bold red lips, stop sign red. A man shows her an 8 x 10 he took of her. In the photo, floating beside her are two flares of light. She points to them and says, "Those are spirits of my Masters." The camcorder follows Neva into her bedroom. On a shelf sits a framed photo of the first Western Master. At the head of her bed, from a ring suspended from the ceiling, bells a sheer white canopy. It looks like a bride's veil, spreading out on either side of the snow white bed. Neva's pillow is metallic silver, shaped like a star. The camera is wonderfully voyeuristic, scanning the row of white outfits hanging in the closet, peeking into her bathroom. It's ordinary, but I imagine her in the tub, performing bubbly rituals involving sea salt, crystals and blue lasers. On Facebook I post a screenshot of the star-shaped pillow.

I reopen Ned's drawing, caress the sharp fold lines bisecting Neva's body. It's titillating, as if the paper has captured a spark of her. I love how amateurish the image is, like a fan's tribute. That's how I feel before Neva, like a fan, enamored of her grandeur, her appetite, her petite ballsiness, her unstoppability. Drinking in Neva, I somehow become more than just Dodie, a mousy ordinary mortal. Neva's hyperreal presence brings out the Jovian nascent in all of us. I long to smoke a Marlboro Menthol, to taste her. She had a stroke a few years ago. I watch a video of a suddenly old Neva. Her left hand curls, clawlike, in the lap of her white crushed velvet jogging suit. I fastforward to a segment that shows her feet. Comfortable white moccasins. Her hair has been trimmed to a chic white pixie, which makes her ears look huge, pearls dangling from lobes. Her mouth opens wide as she talks, and she pulls her lips back, revealing an expanse of even white teeth. "You love each other just because you are," she says. Her post-stroke speech is round and slow, and surprisingly more Southern than before. The left side of her mouth raises into a slight snarl as she says the stroke surprised her, but as Soul she chose it. "In the reality of Soul, there is no good or bad. Everything is important to the process of learning."

The Teacher fixes the student a cup of rooibos tea, then squats down and opens the dorm-sized refrigerator in the corner—his white chinos pull tight across his ass and thighs—and retrieves a carton of half and half. "My one indulgence," he laughs. They take their usual positions, on either side of his large wooden desk. The Teacher says, "I have something for you." From a drawer in his desk he pulls out a book and hands it to her. A thin, hardcover volume, Giorgio Agamben's *Profanations*. "For me, really?" "I thought you might find it interesting—his concept of the daimon." "I don't know what to say, thank you, thank you." The Teacher's eyes sparkle as he gently laughs. "Promise me you'll let me know what you think of it." "I will! I'll read it cover to cover, I'll study it, I'll let you know!" The phone rings, and the Teacher picks up the receiver. Some business about an upcoming retreat. Trying not to eavesdrop, the student examines a silver framed photo on his desk—of a man holding a pistol to his head and smirking. The student finds the photo confusing—though the picture's a bit fuzzy she recognizes the man; it's the guru who founded their sect. The Teacher hangs up the phone and nods toward the photo. "A reminder to not take myself too seriously. Guruji had a great sense of humor." He smiles sweetly, then falls silent. It isn't a passive silence, it's a test to see if she can rest there with him, in the moment. The student awkwardly sips her milky tea, waiting. Finally he says, "Being the Teacher is very lonely, always having to project a calm, professional demeanor." He looks down at his hands. "No one really knows me." He looks up at her with big amber doe eyes. "It's such a treat with you," he says. "We're just two sentient beings sharing a cup of tea. Sharing ourselves." The student smiles broadly, her solar plexus fluttering. The Teacher gets up and walks her to the door. His body moves with an elegance at once feral and controlled.

Any guru worth his salt insists, "Don't take my word for it. Believe only what you personally experience." This is one of history's biggest come-ons. Truth is, we're conditioned to experience anything we're told. In her study of super-Nazi Adolf Eichmann, Hannah Arendt theorizes that Eichmann wasn't born evil. Initially he was repelled by the death camps, as any normal person would be. How long did it take Eichmann to overcome that repugnance and become an efficient bureaucrat in the Nazi extermination machine? How long did it take him to revision mass killing as a heroic task? Four weeks. When you enter a new belief system, tiny lines are crossed and crossed and crossed—it may look from the outside that you've made a huge leap—but from the inside there are all these incremental … steps … and you have no idea how you went from sociologist sent to study an extraterrestrial cult … to standing outside in the snow with your fellow believers, clad only in plastic and polyester, eager for Ro of Varna to appear from the sky. Alison Lurie's *Imaginary Friends*: "I still knew rationally that the Varnians weren't coming, since they didn't exist; but I felt, if only through empathy, the emotion appropriate to such an event, and the intense pressure of the group will that it should happen. My heart was beating hard." One day I'm joking about shamanism and four weeks later I'm in a circle with thirty other former doubters who are grunting and screeching, and I'm hopping up and down so that a frog spirit can use my body to enter the middle world. We'll believe any system we're immersed in. When I took a long-term temp job at Pacific Gas and Electric, *I'm* not a secretary, I told myself, I'm the kind of person who *has* secretaries. Within two months I'm hiding out in the cubicle of a woman from Fremont, hanging on every detail of her recent trip to Sears to buy workpants for her husband, and when I hear there's a full-time opening, I'm asking lifers how likely it would be for a temp to get it. This is why I will never be a charismatic. As far as reality goes, the charismatic calls the shots and the world conforms. When Neva says that whatever you imagine IS, she's trying to teach us to be like her. But that's not possible. As a charismatic leader, she is a different species from the rest of us. She could sense that from an early age, her lack of human doubt, and thus Nikwuz was born. I am full of doubt, my psyche malleable as plastic, and over and over I've tried to dig myself deeper into soul-destroying muck. There's something about being on the bottom rung of any system that makes me want to climb, aesthetics and self-preservation be damned. In 1981, a couple of years after I moved to San Francisco, I quit writing poetry because I took on the belief that narrative poetry was bad, that straightforward poetry was bad. I could see that writing it wouldn't get me anywhere, so I got all experimental and prosey. I took on New Narrative's tenets with the same uncritical zeal as I did the cult's. There were two Masters, and I devoted enormous amounts of energy trying to please them, in my writing, in my aesthetic consumption, in my social life, in my display of sexual appetite. Like the students of any other cult, I desperately defended my place in the inner circle of the Masters. Like them, I felt superior to those not in the inner circle. I was jealous and insecure, and the Masters were fickle with their affections. After a time I became irritated that no matter what was being discussed, there was an official version—what the Masters believed—and I wanted to insert my opinion into the mix. It is at this point that the Medieval Catholic cult would excommunicate and/or burn an uppity heretic. My novel *The Letters of Mina Harker* began as a cult document, but ultimately traces a rebellion against doctrine. It is the text of a body at war. When I was a child I was taught I was ugly, too ugly to ever be loved, and I'm still trying to figure out what to do about that, still trying to figure out how to kill off the abused girl I carry around inside of me, how to load her on a bus and crash it, and out of the gasoline flames arise as a new self born of wisdom and love.

Staring at the image of anything with the right focus, a human will have "inner" or spiritual experiences with it. Like his students, filmmaker/fake guru Kumaré closes his eyes and experiences the blue light, even though he made up the blue light. The blue light was a meditation we did in the cult. The blue light was the light of the Master; when you saw the blue light it was confirmation the Master was always with you. I had more inner experiences with Molly, my cat, than with the Master. I once dreamt Molly was a bank teller, and this was a profoundly spiritual dream for me. Molly behind the bank teller plate glass, standing on a chair, her front paws on the counter, an avatar of Soul. Neva says, "My mission for being here is to remind people of things that this mind has no way to remember. But you know it as Soul. Your Soul knows all of this. It's nothing new. You're just being reminded." For any system to survive it must become self-perpetuating. In the movie *Bug,* the crucial point is when Ashley Judd's psychotic boyfriend tells her she has the key to the mystery of where the bugs came from. "Where did the bugs come from?" he asks. "I don't know I don't know," she cries. "You do know, put it together, the pieces fit." "They don't fit, I don't know." "They do fit, you have to look harder. Start from the beginning." Ashley squints her eyes and remembers the grocery store where her son was abducted, then slowly she starts generating her own buggy logic. Soon she's hopping up and down shouting, "They gave me the queen. I am the super mother bug!" A moment of true conversion, or what they call in Buddhism dharma transmission, is not something you learn, it's something you catch. In 1976, when Joni Mitchell met Trungpa Rinpoche, he asked her, "Do you believe in God?" Joni replied, "Yes, here's my god and here is my prayer," and she snorted some cocaine. As he watched her, Trungpa Rinpoche began to breathe rhythmically, his nostrils flaring like bellows. "What's with his nose?" Joni thought. His breathing was hypnotic, and when she left she felt changed. "For three days I had no sense of self, no self-consciousness; my mind was back in Eden, the mind before the Fall. It was simple-minded, blessedly simple-minded. And then the 'I' came back, and the first thought I had was, Oh, my god. He enlightened me." Enlightenment leapt from Rinpoche's nostrils into Joni's heart. She quit cocaine and began writing songs about the guru.

The next time the student visits his office, there's something the Teacher wants to tell her. "People who've known me thirty years don't know this." Their eyes lock soulfully. "This is something I've only told lovers and therapists, yet somehow I feel I can trust you." His intimate tone so startles the student she sloshes a bit of rooibos tea on her lap. "You *can* trust me," she says. "You mustn't tell anyone." "I won't." His mother was killed in a drive-by when he was eighteen. "I'd been fighting with her before I left for college"—he snaps his fingers—"and then she was gone. I'm terrified of abandonment, because it's like a death to me." He holds the student's gaze for what feels like minutes, totally open, unguarded, amber eyes moistening. Finally she looks down at her teacup. It is embossed with a gold-leaf OM sign. An irregular rust-colored blotch stains her white gauze skirt. The Teacher says, "Tell me about *your* childhood." She talks on and on, about her verbally abusive father, her emotionally distant mother, her outsiderness, her alienation from her body. The Teacher listens intently. When she gets up to leave, they linger in the doorway. "Your friendship means the world to me," he says. Her clit clenches so tightly it aches. How could she be such a dirty girl, how could she defile this beautiful chaste thing they have together. She longs to hug him, but she dare not. She finds herself masturbating daily, sometimes twice a day, to relieve the terrible pressure. Each time she fantasizes giving the Teacher a blowjob. She can't imagine him doing anything to her debased body—but if he did, it would be the most loving, transcendent experience of her life, she has no doubt about that. She envisions the Teacher sitting in his desk chair. He says to her gently, "Time to milk me." The student kneels down and takes his powerful rockhard cock in her mouth. When he/she comes she always swallows his semen. The next time they meet in real life, the Teacher tells her another painful secret from childhood, which she cherishes. He admits he's never before felt such an intense connection with a student. They must be careful with each other, he warns, not to get hooked.

Anyone can become a wisdom-generating machine. I read Kevin Sutra 73: *I loved making all those films, even the bad ones.* "What does it mean?" I ask. He shrugs his shoulders and says, "If you can't cut the mustard, get out of the kitchen?" I smirk and say, "Be serious. *I loved making all those films, even the bad ones.* What's the interpretation of the sutra?" "To accept all your experiences." "Precisely!" I shout. I've watched so many videos of Neva, I could generate new Jovian dogma. My body dissolves into a rainbow of colored radiations—I say, because of all those clouds and gasses, Jovians don't get much sunlight and that's why our skin is so pale, our hair so blonde. I add a diamond-crusted thunderbolt necklace to my outfit, and laugh more to demonstrate a *jovial* energetic field. I talk about how Chris Farley was Jovian, but he wasn't strong enough to handle the dense negativity of the lower worlds. The interlunar council staged his death so he could return to Jupiter. He's been reunited with his Jovian family and is doing just fine. Jovians have infiltrated humanity through the ages, I explain—great innovators in all fields. You can recognize them by the prominence of the letter N in their names, for the energy of N aids us in harmonizing with your planet—Isaac Newton, Nancy Sinatra, Neil Armstrong, Ellen DeGeneres, Leonardo da Vinci, Abraham Lincoln, Richard Nixon, John Lennon, Zora Neale Hurston, Raymond Pettibon, Jon Bon Jovi, Thandie Newton, Wassily Kandinsky, Benjamin Franklin, Benito Mussolini, Denzel Washington, Princess Diana, David Niven, Anais Nin, Nina Simone, Ogden Nash, Hermann Goering, Arnold Schwarzenegger, Morgan Freeman, Alan King, Dean Martin, and Antonio Banderas. John Coltrane, Ornette Coleman, and Coleman Hawkins are all from the same Jovian family. Many, many poets are from Jupiter, including Anne Waldman, Ron Silliman, Ntozake Shange, Lyn Hejinian, Trinh T. Minh-ha, Allen Ginsberg, Countee Cullen, John Wieners, Justin Chin, Kevin Killian, Ariana Reines, Lorna Dee Cervantes, Gwendolyn Brooks, and Brandon Brown. When Chris Farley, whose Jovian name is Nykur, came to Earth, he was 127 Jovian years old, a mere child. He hadn't received the requisite number of initiations for Earth inhabitation, but he was so eager to raise the consciousness of mankind, the Spiritual Fathers made an exception. Because of his lack of thorough preparation, Farley was never confident in his ability to blend in with Earthlings, and he chose an N-free Earth name in order to hide his extraterrestrial roots. Sadly, this was a tragic mistake—one that a more seasoned Jovian would never have made.

Things I've done since the cult: I took psychic development classes from a Russian woman who claimed to be the niece of Sergei

Diaghilev; talked to psychics on the phone; saw a psychic in person to have my chakras cleared, twice a month for a full year. I took weekly Hatha yoga classes and series on the Yoga Sutras—when we were assigned to choose a yama or niyama and practice it, I chose for the week to not say tacky things about people, and failed miserably. I studied mindfulness meditation at Kaiser Permanente, attended a meditation group at the Sausalito public library, did a weekend with Pema Chodron. I wrote a book about an affair with a Buddhist teacher who never discussed Buddhism with me. I attended a dharma seminar in Tiburon. I visited the Hartford Street and Page Street and Upaya zendos. I read goddess books, Jungian books, saw a Jungian therapist who was always pushing freeze dried garlic capsules on me, why I can't remember. I got tarot readings, took workshops in Shamanism, went to a Shamanic therapist who had me pilgrimage to Golden Gate Park to find a stick which I then wrapped with yarn and feathers while listening to recorded drums. She had a PhD in psychology, so Blue Cross paid a portion of her $175 an hour fee. A therapist in Mill Valley inspired the *TV Sutras*. She told me to meditate and do yoga at home, and somehow I obeyed. I'd walk past her huge curvy swimming pool with its bright turquoise water, sit on a couch in the pool house and wait for her. She'd sit in a wicker chair, facing me. I'd be sweating like a pig from the hot Marin summer, but she was always crisp in her linen pants and blouses that revealed enough wrinkled cleavage to make me uncomfortable. She was writing a book herself, with her husband; she hated writing but she did it because her husband pressured her. When I talked about my frustration with writing, she'd tell me that writing was really,

really hard. She said I should quit teaching and get a job in a coffee house. When I had a good week, she'd remind me how exhausting it is to take care of myself, how lonely I must really feel. I was sick a lot, and she said I needed to accept I may never get well. She'd been in a cult herself, for thirty years, a psychology cult. It's hard to leave a cult, she said. Each week I'd return home feeling undercut and demeaned, but it wasn't until I looked up her cult that I bolted. The followers believed they were going to change the planet with their spiritual psychology principles. After the founder was accused of giving his daughter LSD and raping her, the group disintegrated, but my therapist remained loyal. I've juice fasted, cleansed, been stuck with acupuncture needles, had chiropractic adjustments and Tibetan internal organ massages, consulted three different ayurvedic practitioners, downed herbs vitamins and amino acids. At the Jack Tar Hotel I saw a trance channeler who spoke with a brogue, and at the Masonic Auditorium I saw John Edward, the TV psychic who talks to the dead. I saw Trungpa Rinpoche's son and when I went up to get his book signed, he stared into my eyes as if I were the only person in the world, and I thought *he's really good at what he does*. I saw Swami Satchidananda, went to group therapy for eating disorders in Marin for five years, attended a Genene Roth weekend in Redwood City where I learned how food addiction could lead me to love and spiritual awakening. I saw a New Age therapist who performed an exorcism to remove my demons, and another therapist whose thing is ADHD, and he talked me into taking Ritalin. I lost all access to pleasure, started staying up all night, engaging in frantic tweaker behaviors. I felt so desperate, alien, out of control, I googled

Ritalin and demonic possession. After I collapsed with vertigo onto my kitchen floor, I quit both therapist and drug, cold turkey. In my commentaries to the *TV Sutras* I am generating the logic of absorbed systems. Not observation, absorption.

I sit cross-legged and hold a lotus seed mala in my right hand (the wrong hand), and I take one in and one out breath per bead. Four rounds (108 beads/in and out breaths per round) is a full meditation for me. Two rounds is a quickie. When I'm frazzled from spending too much time online, I need five rounds. *In breath out breath* suddenly I'm thinking of Jeannette Winterson's memoir, her attempts to write the best book ever *in breath out breath* some reviewers found the egotism of this insufferable *in breath out breath* I have always wanted to write the best book ever *in breath* as if there were shame in being plain and just getting the ideas out there *out breath* do I still need to be part of an avant-garde *in breath out breath in breath out breath* no longer am I sure what is surface, what is depth. Walking through the city, I see hunched bundles of loneliness, persons who feel unloved, unworthy, all wrong. Behind the blandest face huge emotional dramas rage—the charismatic really gets that, the charismatic is willing to reach in there and touch the untouchable, the charismatic isn't picky like I am about whose love they will accept. Kevin and I were on the bus recently and there was a guy on a corner, yelling and throwing his body around—the kind of behavior that I'd cross the street to avoid—he was walking away from Mission, down 7th Street, and this preppy guy ran after him, and through the guy's flailing and yelling, pressed some money into his hand. Kevin and

I were both stunned. The crazy guy paused for a moment, looked at the money, then started yelling and throwing his arms about. He couldn't help it. After four mala rounds I feel like a different person, as if layers of crud have melted from my brain—and my synapses, like ratty hair that's been combed, flow smoothly. The is-ness of the room I'm sitting in touches me. Sometimes when I'm cross-legged I feel ancient, like I'm a tuning fork and this is how the original humans were taught to reset their bio-machines, and at that moment I totally can believe they were taught by visitors from other worlds. Sometimes I imagine that we're all living in an elaborate computer game and alien beings are watching us for fun and leisure, the way we watch reality shows on TV—and the end of the world that all these religions are predicting simply means the game is over and somebody presses the reset button.

During meditation practice, the Teacher touches my back, gently correcting my alignment. The heat from his hand enlivens me. Afterwards he takes me aside and says, "There were dozens of bodies in that room, but you're the only one that listened to me." The Teacher can tell how I'm feeling just from the sound of my footsteps approaching the meditation hall. My Teacher and I talk daily, sometimes two or three times a day. Besides spirituality, we discuss politics, literature, and postmodern theory. All phenomena, he tells me, are worthy of study. I can't deny my desire for the Teacher, this deep connection I feel for him—I feel it, dammit, this deep, painful, useless love that I don't want or approve of, that I keep trying to make go away, but it won't go, it grows stronger each day. The Teacher remains reserved, though nakedly honest about his personal shyness and isolation. He tells me that sex is joyfully using another and allowing oneself to be used. Some days my Teacher is maddening and I want to flee, other times he is tender and my heart chakra spirals open. My Teacher rails against idiot compassion that enables another in their foolishness. He tells me that sex with the proper person, with the proper attitude, can open new layers of enlightenment. My Teacher exudes so much energy, I'm afraid if I were ever to touch him, really touch him, I'd be fried alive. I pulled a tarot card about him—it was the Death card, which means that only through approaching my Teacher with the innocent acceptance of a child can I be spared. My Teacher confessed that he's very lonely. Always being the one others turn to, who can he turn to? If only he had one person to understand him, to hold the fullness of him. He looked so sad and alone, yet strong, so powerful, I wanted to cradle him in my arms until we both felt joyous, with tears in our eyes, innocent tears. Sometimes I feel like a nasty girl, like I'm violating him when I jerk off.

Neil tells me he's doing a life-size painting of a tree on which the Virgin Mary appeared. In 1988, a week before Christmas, in Neil's hometown—Sulphur, Louisiana—street lights cast a shadow through the large waxy leaves of a 30-year-old magnolia tree, and the Virgin Mary materialized on the trunk. Each night hundreds of people came to visit the apparition, which rose up the tree, three feet high. When I ask if it really looked like the Virgin Mary, Neil says, "No. Everyone brings their own Virgin Mary." The next day he emails me two jpegs. I open the first, a distressed photo whose colors have faded and shifted to turquoise, rust, tan. On the tree trunk, I see a blob of light. Nothing more. The second jpeg is a news clip from Associated Press. The tree's owner, John New, age 46, tells an unnamed reporter, "It looks as though she is pregnant, just as she would have been at this time of year." His wife, Mary New, age 59, says, "It's a miracle. I think she is here to warn us to have peace in the world and for the whole nation to understand one another." I look at the photo again, and suddenly on the turquoise and tan tree trunk the white blob coalesces into a pregnant woman in three-quarters profile. Her eye is cast downward, and her lips curve in a beneficent, serene smile. The Virgin and a patch of white ground around the tree glow, as if she were emerging from the earth and climbing the tree—or melting and flowing back into the earth. The glowing white looks like snow—unlikely for Louisiana—the glowing white looks infrared, the white heat of Mary's holiness, love.

In one of the Secrets of the Universe Revealed videos on YouTube, a "scientist" claims that we're living in a black hole. He says, look outside at night, what do you see? It's dark out. That's because it's a black hole. Eight-year-old Dodie lying on her twin bed, staring out the window at the vast blackness of space, my little heart fluttering with awe and terror. Neva: "We experience the darkness, but we're light in the darkness." In the cult we ate meat because the animals chose to give themselves to mankind for nourishment. We loved the animals as we ate them. Like Neva did with her stroke, the animals chose. All the horrible things in her life, my life, the animals' lives, we chose them. Our suffering is necessary for raising the vibration of the planet. Since the early 80s the cult has been normalizing and mainstreaming. That is the trajectory of all cults. The original wild charismatic leader dies or whatever, replaced by a committee that regiments the doctrine. The formation of a cult is expansive, whereas its perpetuation is contractive. The miraculous generosity of Christ versus the Crusades or fundamentalist abortion clinic bombers. Neva is a throwback to the cult's early days, when we valued quirkiness, individualism, permission. In every online video, Neva says don't let anybody tell you how to be, how to act. Of course the cult always told its members how to think, but it didn't used to be so obvious. Through Neva I tap into why I fell in love with the cult. Soul is immortal and there is nothing to fear death is just a stage a new beginning love fuels the universe. An innocent girl in touch with Soul can walk through dangerous neighborhoods and nobody will bother her because she has the Master's protection. She sees the people there as Soul, not as killers thieves rapists, and the treacherous hooded masses part for her as she skips by, beaming love. If we think frightened thoughts, the world will be scary. If we think positive thoughts, we will live in abundance and harmony. God created everything in non-ending cycles because god loves itself. We each have the ability to create because we are a part of god, who loves every single part of itself. God is the original charismatic narcissist.

One summer in Bloomington, Nance and I separated for a couple of months. I moved into a slum apartment house on the town square. The Bloomington Gay Alliance was located upstairs. Occasionally the building was overtaken with huge wild parties that BGA advertised in the school paper. It was expected if you wanted to sleep on those nights you'd crash elsewhere. Other residents taught me how to break into vacated units with a butter knife, in order to score abandoned furniture. Thus I managed to acquire a twin bed, dresser, and some metal shelves—plenty for my one room "efficiency." See me in the twin bed, beneath a lavender printed Indian bedspread, lying on my side, naked with this guy named Mark, who I met earlier that evening at the Student Union Building. If you look across the street at the clock tower of the courthouse, you'll see it's 10:15. The open window lets in a whiff of jasmine and the thumping of country rock from the Bluebird, the best bar in town. Mark has the thoughtlessly toned body of a 1970s twenty-something. Nobody but sports freaks worked out back then. With his clear eyes, shaggy brown curls, you'd never guess he was a Hare Krishna. He showed me a picture of himself in an apricot-colored robe and shaved head, small glob of paint in the space between his eyes. Like pigeons, Hare Krishnas gathered in public places, chanting "Hare Krishna, Hare Krishna, Krishna Krishna, Hare Hare Hare Rama, Hare Rama, Rama Rama, Hare Hare" and offering free food. I'd heard that followers were fed lots of sugar to keep them high. Beatle George Harrison was a Hare Krishna before people knew better. I'm thinking of Mark because of the fellow I met last night in Bed Bath & Beyond. I asked the sales woman if they had any down and feather pillows and a guy standing nearby—wirerims, short yellow-white hair, pasty—handed me one, saying that's the very pillow he was buying. "I'm an expert in this department," he quipped. He wore an Indian tunic of sheer white cotton, his aura simultaneously anal and hippiesh. I shopped for a bit then took the escalator back down to the first floor, where I bumped into him again, and we laughed about it, and then, several minutes later, we happened to walk out the door at the same time. "Don't follow me home," he joked. I put my pillows in the car trunk, then sauntered over to Trader Joe's. In the frozen food aisle, there he was. We both laughed heartily. In the frosty fluorescent light, his pale eyes looked transparent, insubstantial, as if they were mere projections of eyes. Between them were teeny blobs of paint—a white dash, a couple of yellow dots—in a vertical line. He was putting out a flirtatious vibe I wasn't interested in, yet I felt oddly comfortable. He said, since we kept running into each other he might as well give me a flyer. "I just moved up from San Diego and I'm opening a Bikram yoga center." He shoved a xeroxed sheet of yellow paper at me. "Oh thanks," I said, dropping it into my bright red Trader Joe's basket, and moving on. At home I looked up the website, and sure enough, the guy was a Hare Krishna. I knew they still existed because I saw a few bald-headed guys in pale orange robes shopping together at the Whole Foods in Venice. They looked like Martians, but they talked and acted like the other Whole Foods shoppers, discussing the merits of this brand of croutons over the other.

Mark had escaped from the group several months before and was hiding out. I found it exciting to sleep with someone on the run. Mark said he'd been in an arranged marriage with a woman he didn't know, and they were only supposed to have sex during certain times of the month. The men wore "Brahmin underwear," a white cloth that was bound tightly around their balls to suppress sexual desire, but he and his wife enjoyed their sex and were guiltily going at it all the time. Having snuck sex with Nance since grade school, I understood the charge and trauma of forbidden encounters, two innocents carving out pleasure where none was allowed—but my cult was nothing like Mark's cult, my cult was normal, based on love, we didn't have weird sexual restrictions, we didn't live together in groups, there were no scandals, no lies. Damage wafted off of Mark like a scent. He was terrified the Hare Krishnas would find him. When he talked about them he lowered his voice to a whisper. I'm so glad I didn't sleep with the Hare Krishna at Trader Joe's. I didn't desire him, but somehow it still feels like I escaped, like those women who when Ted Bundy, arm in sling, came knocking, didn't open the door. In the late 70s, when I moved to San Francisco, my apartment was down the street from a Moonie compound, and the way they tried to reel you in was to compliment you on your outfit, then invite you over for dinner. Every time I left the house I had to scamper through a gauntlet of "Nice blouse, nice jacket." Cults are like the quicksand we imagined in the linoleum in my grade school hallways; you have to step carefully on the dark stripes in the pattern, for with one missed step you'll slip into a grainy beige abyss. The most dangerous patch was right outside the cafeteria.

When I google "Hare Krishnas + scandal," the results are really bad. In the year 2000, 44 former students of their boarding schools sued the organization for child physical and sexual abuse. Other allegations include drug dealing, weapons stockpiling, and murder. Children slept on concrete floors, got up at 4 a.m. to take cold showers, chanting Sanskrit prayers. Breakfast consisted of cold oatmeal, often tainted with cockroaches that the kids called "flying dates." Children trudged through snow and rain with little clothing on. Children were sent to massage and bathe the gurus who lived among them, and afterwards they drank the "blessed" water in which the men had been sitting. Children were lined up and beaten with flyswatters and tree branches. Children were scrubbed with steel wool, locked in closets and cupboards crawling with rats. Children were forced to drink "sacred" cow urine and to bathe in cow manure. Children who spilt their milk were forced to lick it off the floor. Children were forced to eat their vomit. Young girls were blindfolded and stripped and told they were going to see the doctor, and then they were raped. Boys were forced to give blow jobs. Boys were sodomized at knife-point. I'd like to say these are the worst cult travesties I've read about, but they're not.

Walking to the meditation center, I felt blissful. I passed a strip of corporate garden—tall stalks of plants with rows of bell-shaped flowers. The colors—purples, pinks, yellows—were so vivid I could barely stand it. Across the street, high in the air, three intense blue flags. I thought about what my Teacher said about radical acceptance. I feel enormous desire for him, and I'm afraid of that. I don't want anything physical. That's an impossibility. My Teacher would never want me. All this arousal based on so little, these few conversations about life and meaning. I'm sure he's not feeling any of these ways about me. I feel so foolish. Accepting that foolishness,

I suppose, is part of radical acceptance. Is it possible to proceed with an open heart without expectation? Are my girlish fantasies a form of expectation? I have not flirted with him—never would I flirt with my Teacher—so hopefully he doesn't suspect anything. Sometimes these rushes of erotic energy seem to come from outside myself. Sometimes it's more diffuse than that—it's like I feel his being. More than words are happening between us—I feel as if he is channeling his heart directly to me. Am I delusional? Am I a silly adolescent romantic? When my Teacher embraced me, he had such powerful, clean energy. He said softly, "You have a spirit of gold that I need to learn from." I feel so embarrassed and humiliated, fear that I am failing him. I keep thinking about the child on the Death card, being innocent before the transformative energy, not resisting it or getting the ego involved.

In Bloomington, the one other guy I'd taken back to my efficiency apartment was appalled. He took in the sink just a few feet away from the bed, the closet-sized bathroom in the corner, the peeling paint, dull wooden floor, and said, "How could you live in a dump like this." And then he left. But Mark seemed comfortable there, I'm sure he could have done with much less. We talked through the night. I told him there were many paths to God, that he joined the Hare Krishnas because it matched his level of vibration. But now that he left them he had new vibrations, and maybe he should consider my cult. He was so gentle and sad. Sex did happen but what I remember is the atmosphere of a pajama party, two peas in footed jammies sharing secrets. Soon afterwards I moved back in with Nance. Life without her was more exciting, but I was simply and brutally incapable of being alone. I had been with her since I was eleven. When other teens were individuating, I fused. Nance took care of all my emotional needs. If I was upset, she talked me down; if I was insecure, she built me up. Without her, my moods raged, fear so intense it felt like there was a horse inside my solar plexus bucking its way out. I'm fascinated with girls who have been held captive in basements and backyard compounds. When I hear of a new one, I lose days online gorging on their ordeals. Girls buffered from the outside world, girls who have no choice but to love their captors, girls who fully appreciate small pleasures, who treat spiders as pets, girls who have never dated or gone to a prom or had their heart broken, girls who have never been laughed at, girls who pass up opportunities to flee—the captor is all you know, the captor never betrays you—pale stunted girls who live through hell but end up thirty years old and innocent as butter. I am not these girls, but like Mark I know there is an otherness from which you will never ever be released.

Nance moves through this writing like a shadow. I can't bear to think of her. The last time I saw her, which was in the late 80s, she put out this "she was spiritual and I was negative" vibe. She said she'd developed the ability to see colors, and by these colors she could divine the energy of something. Like if she looks at an entree on a restaurant menu and she sees red, she knows she should avoid that item. I'd sent her some recent work and she said my writing was very intense, that reading it evoked colors she usually doesn't see, like gray and maroon. In the cult's elaborate spiritual color symbology, gray and maroon are so far off the register, they aren't even mentioned. "So what about the cult," I said, wanting to slap her. For a number of years her interest waned, but when she received a slip in the mail for her fifth initiation—a total surprise—she recommitted. Becoming a higher initiate made her realize that leadership was her calling. She was in town to deliver a keynote speech at a pyramid marketing convention for an herbal tonic. She was a top distributor, which meant she inspired lots and lots of people to buy and sell the concoction. She was taking leadership workshops with people who impressed her, top corporate executives, and she felt a special affinity with Martin Luther King because they both were Capricorns. Her longtime girlfriend, Bett, was with her. They ate the same foods, worked and played together, had the same friends opinions clothing style; they wore matching gold bands and slung around the word "we" as if it were the only pronoun they knew. "The relationship takes precedence over everything," Nance said. Witnessing their fusion was like watching a biopic about myself, except that the actress playing me lacked my spunk. Bett didn't even have her own job, working instead as Nance's assistant on corporate consulting projects. "We design learning modules for Symantec." They did everything together, and Nance got all the credit. She'd tell anyone who'd listen that Bett's input was major, but nobody did listen. I took them to Osenta, the women's hot tubs in the Mission. The three of us naked in a scalding vat—somehow I thought this was a good idea. Bett seemed nice. I could tell she thought Nance was behaving like a jerk. Bett isn't in the cult, which must be her one small pocket of rebellion. "Everyone thinks of Bett as a cultist," Nance said, her Dixie cup breasts hovering above the steaming waterline. When we parted, she gave me a bottle of herbal tonic. "Try this. I think it will make a big difference." We're Facebook friends but we never message each other. In the photos of her and other middle-aged lesbians with short-cropped hair, she looks happy.

The Teacher moves his chair to her side of the desk, so that they're facing each other. He leans forward and says, "You seem strangely familiar, as if we've known one another in a past life." The student swallows her rooibos tea. "Yes, me too." Staring deeply into her eyes he asks what she thinks of the word "desire," and she daringly tells him she's been feeling a lot of desire lately. "When did this desire begin?" he asks, with a just a hint of smile. "Since I started talking with you," she blurts out, voice quivering, tears in eyes. He scoots his chair closer and puts his arms around her. As she sobs he says, "I've been having similar feelings." She finds herself wailing, "I can't stand it, I want you." The Teacher kisses her gently on the cheek, close to her mouth. The student grabs his lips with her lips. He doesn't resist.

A betrayal puts me in touch with my vulnerability, my brute confrontations with loss. I watch a DVD of a cultist with terminal cancer. She says her impending death is good for her practice because she really *gets* impermanence. She says she's happier than others around her because her eyes are wide open, drinking in the wonders of the world. Her eyes are painful to look at, bright yellow from jaundice. In the TV show *Enlightened,* the camera focuses on close-ups of brilliant roses to signal Laura Dern's moments of spiritual connection, calm. It's totally cheesy yet I recognize the feeling, where the gorgeousness of nature pops in sharp relief. Sometimes the glory of nature will expand to include nearby humans, sometimes not. In Developing the Novel my vision shifts and suddenly the students appear precious, all that life coursing through them, their tender hopes and fears. I feel like something in me has twirled open, kind of stoned. Back at home I'm sitting on the toilet facing Quincey, who is hunched over her bowl eating, and I can feel the life force coursing through her as well, and I think *We are programmed for ecstasy. Nobody owns that.*

The Teacher warns her about being too forward, too yang. "Little seedlings wilt and die from too much direct sunlight too soon," he says. Yes, he loves her, but they must find the correct exposure for their love. Originally in Chinese, yin meant the shady side of the hill, and yang meant the sunny side. His fingertips lightly touching her shoulder, he says that Western culture is way too yang. She and he should venerate the shady, the hidden, the coy, the not-direct, the slow growing, the careful step by step.

When I made corporate slide shows for a living, my former boss, Gus, told how he was once called before a congressional committee on truth in advertising. For a canned soup campaign, to make the soup look bubbly they filled the bowl with marbles. The congressional committee said this was a lie. Bubbly soup has to really bubble. No more marbles. Gus warned that when we set up photo props we had to be very careful it was what you see is what you get. When I was a child I had a little white sailor hat, with some plastic cherries attached to the front. Across the brim was embroidered "Life is just a bowl of cherries." My grandmother gave it to me. I asked her, what does this mean, how is life like a bowl of cherries? She couldn't tell me. I put on the hat and tap danced across grandma's linoleum floor just like Shirley Temple. We all want cherries, but Teacher after Teacher serves up marbles. The devil and a friend of his were walking down the street, when they saw a man stoop down and pick up something from the ground, look at it, and put it away in his pocket. The friend said to the devil, "What did that man pick up?" "He picked up a piece of the truth," said the devil. "That is a very bad business for you, then," said his friend. "Oh, not at all," the devil replied, "I am going to help him organize it."

Three in the morning, I sit at my computer in a sleeveless knit nightgown, an elongated rectangle stitched at the sides; at the shoulders the material has been gathered and twisted, causing the front of the gown to fall in soft drapes that remind me of the gown of a Grecian goddess. Unwashed, a bit smelly, hair mussed, groggy, listless, unspeakably alone, goddess gown cascading across the Aeron chair I bought used on Craig's List, I watch video after video of Neva, most of which I've seen before. When she enters a room, dullness flies out the window. Everybody knows something is happening, everyone feels remarkably alive and they believe this is their natural state, to be remarkably alive. Neva is a catalyst for our own aliveness. All charismatics are. I roll my eyes at Neva's simplistic generalities, her stagy white hair and clothes. I have no doubt she's a fraud, a con artist, yet I love her. I love her passion and conviction, the way she never contradicts herself, the ludicrous explanations she comes up with when cornered. With her unwavering razor-sharp focus, who wouldn't want her gaze turned on them? When Neva is around we're locked into the present, for no other moment could possibly be as vivid as this one. Neva is bigger than life and as long as we're synched with her, we are too. As long as. When I broke up with my Buddhist Teacher lover the worst part—worse than missing him—was returning to ordinary. Charismatics are addictive, they count on that. The student comes back again and again to suck sweet nectar from the Teacher's teat. No matter how bizarre the teachings get.

The Teacher locks his office door and says, "At a certain point you open to compassion because it's more fun." Then he unzips his white chinos and pulls out his cock. "This is where the real learning begins." I've never seen a spiritual cock before, it has this magnetic aura around it, like objects could fly across the room and stick to it. The cock energy is so intense, when I look at it my vision blurs and the cock is bathed in golden light, tendrils of cock light curl towards me like golden smoke, awakening my clit. We lie down on the floor, on top of an oriental rug that the Teacher says is invaluable, a relic from the home of Guruji. He pushes my legs up over my head—a sacred tantric position—and on the intricate crimson wool plunges into me, books and banners surrounding us like colorful blessings. I scream in pain. The Teacher says as he thrusts, "Submit to the pain until pain and pleasure are one." And then I feel myself breaking open with light. Afterwards, as I walk home, my heart is so raw the world looks ultraviolet. I give money to the first two begging men

I see. The first man says, "I love you." The other man says, "You're beautiful."

Driving down 7th on a Sunday night, the four lanes are eerily empty. In the middle of the street, a figure totters from lane to lane, wearing a long dress with a sleeveless robe draped over it, like images of Jesus in my Sunday School coloring book. As my car approaches I see it is a young guy, barefoot. He has one arm lifted in front of him, palm outward, a sign that means stop, but also a gesture of blessing made by coloring book Jesus. Inside my car I'm enveloped in a soothing duet by Robert Plant and a female country singer as the guy continues to stumble through the barren urban landscape like a confused prophet. The soundtrack turns the scene into an art film, the flashback in *Sound of My Voice,* when Brit Marling's character arrives from the future and weaves through cars in downtown Los Angeles, wearing nothing but an increasingly soiled sheet draped around her body. From there she goes on to found her own cult. In an interview, Marling said that while making the film, the crew formed a cult. Every cult needs a higher power, she continued, and for their film production company, the story was their higher power. Like the cultists in the movie they believed magic could be created in the most banal of spaces.

My Teacher was talking about how the dead are idealized, made perfect. Does that mean when we idealize another person, we render them dead? We had sex last night. The orgasm was so intense I shattered.

I wear moonstone earrings, I wear an amethyst druzy necklace, an obsidian arrowhead edged with gold, a silver lunula set with three labradorites on a leather cord. I soak my stones in filtered water mixed with a tablespoon of sea salt to clean them, and then on a full moon I leave them overnight on the back porch to charge them. On the new moon I make sure I'm doing whatever it is I wish to bring to fruition that month. I'm trying to make room for pleasure in my life, to find a window of bliss to live in each day. With five fish oil capsules and a half an hour of meditation each morning, I can now focus, can follow through. Meditation gets rid of the static. Instead of bouncing all over the place, it's like my neurons start to flow in one direction, fluidly, like a school of sardines. I'm committed to allowing myself to proceed in a more intuitive fashion—and to enjoy what I do rather than seeing life as a chore. Typing this, desperation washes over me, and sunlight splashes dramatically across my desk. A sutra is a thread of exposition, the absolute minimum that is necessary to hold it together. Sutras are terse, easily memorized, but they are intended to be expanded and explained. I'm reminded of the way that anyone from my past is reduced to a discrete set of images—and one fragment will emerge—the Buddhist Teacher wouldn't tell me when his plane got in—and the commentary machine goes haywire, saying I should have called it quits right then—that that was the moment I should have realized it was impossible. In my commentaries, I push back the date when I should have realized things were impossible with him, earlier and earlier. The sutra process is the opposite of the stasis of accepting things as they are, highlighting instead the instability of knowing.

The Teacher is an amusement park, a place as much as a person. The Teacher's mirrors make you stretchy, tall, squat, repeated over and over; dimmed dramatic lighting renders your freakish contours beautiful. Your self becomes putty. It is so simple to manipulate people, a young Teacher will go insane with that knowledge, complimenting others randomly—looking at a woman's cookbooks and saying of a book they've never heard of before, "That's my favorite ayurvedic cookbook," watching the cookbook owner gush with pride. It takes so little, the teeniest shard of acknowledgement, people are that desperate to be seen. While seeming to give unconditionally, the Teacher creates his own terms, her own map of reality into which you are indoctrinated. The Teacher is so vibrant it is almost impossible not to be drawn in. The biggest mistake you can make is loving the Teacher personally for the Teacher doesn't love *you,* the Teacher beaming love to all from her blog, his podium, loves the love of the masses. What naive, trusting animals we followers are, mimicking their tastes their manners to get it right, to feel valid, loved. Teachers are good in an emergency such as a car accident, remaining calm and focused when everybody else is freaking out, for Teachers perform rather than actually *feeling* feeling. They see themselves as a different species than ordinary humans, a genius a starchild, the reincarnation of a visionary poet channeling the voices of the ages. The writings of a Teacher are mere accessories, for the true art of a Teacher is the performance of himself. The Teacher drops terms and references to theoretical texts without explaining them as if the source needed no explanation, as if it were a holy document that true converts to the sacred intellectual realm will get and nod—while the rest of us poor suckers either look embarrassingly clueless or follow the inner circle and nod along. When you fall away from a Teacher or the Teacher dies, it can come as a shock how dreadful the Teacher's paintings/poems/music/books really are—what seemed like glittering gold, without the Teacher's magic wand, melts to shit. The Teacher knows that human rationality is the biggest fantasy of all. The Teacher sees reality differently—as if he were wearing high-powered night-vision goggles. When you follow a Teacher, you're always trying to find her goggles, but they cannot be found. The Teacher describes the world to you as if you were blind—a world you only catch glimpses of through the Teacher's radiance.

We take our meat out and exercise it, feed it local organic produce, dose it with ginkgo biloba so it will go on longer, be attractive to other meats so we can get sex and better jobs and poetry grants. Some people can get these things with unattractive meat but they have to work harder. During childhood we figure out how our meat works, the limits of the real. If I concentrate I can move my arm but not my doll. To move my doll I concentrate and move my arm and then my arm moves the doll—no connection between mind and doll except love, hate, etc. Childhood fantasy is cute, but we're all supposed to embrace the brute real by a certain age, with the exception of some sort of personified god. The hard part for me as a child was not that God/Jesus existed, but that they were the exception and somehow the Holy Ghost was different from the rest of the ghosts in my closet at night. They never told us what the Holy Ghost did; he was the limp part of the trinity, a vestigial organ growing smaller and weaker—and there were the clouds and the blue skies and the trees and the grass and the flowers and the bushes and the sparrows and blue jays and rabbits and squirrels and ants in my backyard and the park; their colors and their forms were then to me an appetite: a feeling and a love, that had no need of a remoter charm, by thought supplied, or any interest unborrowed from the eye. To get to the park you had to walk over the highway overpass—if you overcame the dizzy raptures of its height and stopped on top of the overpass, leaned over its concrete railing and made your fist go up and down in a pumping motion, trucks would honk at you. Along the far edge of the park ran a stream which smelled of sewage and there were crayfish in there that we would somehow retrieve and put in buckets, their little red claws flailing—and grasshoppers and those bugs that looked like sticks, and daddy-longlegs with their teeny bodies and inch-long threadlike legs. I marveled at the vastness and glory of nature but I longed for the magic of ancient times, dinosaurs and the sky cracking open and God speaking in a human voice—here's the truth about the world, God would say, I love you Dodie, God would say—and I would ask God what happened to the dinosaurs, and God would say we decided to miniaturize, the large muscle mass took too much energy to operate, the large muscle mass was too slow and lumbering—and meat is very expensive to produce. In class, Jason declared that the entire universe has been mapped, that scientists now know where the universe ends—*and what's after that* we all laughed nervously—what's on the other side of the computer generated dome—childish questions that still cause flutters of panic in the middle of the night. Smug cultists mincing around, right palm over left fist, their controlled serenity broadcasting they know that all is illusion; they understand this because they've sat cross-legged for days on end, unmoving, until their knees gave out—they understand the world is illusion and they're okay with that—I don't believe them. I do believe the fundamentalist women who go on dates with Jesus, who set a place at the dinner table for Jesus, invite him to talk directly to their families. Over roast lamb with mint jelly, creamed asparagus, and rhubarb pie, Jesus tells the family the magic never died. Jesus loves lamb with mint jelly.

With female baby boomers turning to spirituality in record numbers—women ignored by their husbands, widowed or otherwise unhappily alone—the populations of fuckable students at spiritual retreats is enormous. And then there's the occasional adoring acolyte in her 20s and early thirties, doe-eyed with lotus tattoo at the base of her spine, just above her ass cheeks. A firm-fleshed delicacy, to be sure. The Teacher reveals nothing about his life, his background. He may be married, he may be single, widowed, divorced, bi: the student never knows. He's a spiritual blank slate totally in the present moment. The Teacher exudes an erotic allure that is never acknowledged; it comes so naturally to him, he barely notices. If asked, he'd call it his life force, the power of being a channel for spirit. The Teacher is upright and proper; he never flirts. Isn't this the very definition of decency? He is well-nigh impeccable in the student's presence, holding his body very still. One couldn't have better decorum in the presence of the Virgin Mary. It is not the Teacher's fault if the student finds this arousing. She always comes on to him, and fucking her the Teacher is merely following the energy of the moment. He's bestowing compassion upon the student. She needs to be fucked. Spirit flows in from his crown chakra, down his spine and into his cock which thrusts the spirit into her cunt. The Teacher whispers into her ear, "As I penetrate you, I penetrate your delusions." With the middle-aged woman he has to use extra lubricant. The fucking is too slippery, but he's able to last forever, and she moans and weeps. It's exhausting. When student and Teacher fuck, it is a symbiotic relationship. He makes her feel chosen and exciting; afterwards she blushes and sparkles during group meditation, legs crossed, her raw cunt a gaping reminder of the most important night of her life. The student makes the Teacher feel potent, like a spiritual rock star.

It's been a year since I've looked at my *TV Sutras,* and I'm worried they're god-awful. When I finally marshal the nerve to read them— *put good in, put good out—you're looking at that moss like it's going to sing to you—all the princes are nothing, nothing—wait for green before driving through tunnel*—they're fine, solid *A Course in Miracles*-type aphorisms, funny, at times inspiring, but plodding and quotidian compared to the swirling auras of my favorite mystical texts. How can I be more extravagant and crazy, how can I enter an ecstatic tradition whose language is so fucking much fun? If I put on the drag of charismatic poet, who would she be? Her name is Azule Linga ... and she's known for her channeled blog, *Blaue Lingua.* In the sidebar, Franz Marc's *Large Blue Horses* is positioned above a looped animation of a blue flame so that it looks like the flame is slowly roasting the Marc's curvy blue beasts. When Azule was a depressed undergrad named something common like Lisa or Ashley, she was shuffling across Sarah Lawrence when a Blue Angel appeared in a crosswalk and touched its blue pointer finger to her forehead. A bolt of spiritual electricity shocked her, and when she looked up she saw a glowing blue light streaming down from the heavens. "This is the Blue Light," the Blue Angel told her. "Henceforth you shall be called Azule Linga. Your life's mission is to write poetry and to channel the Blue Light." The Blue Angel disappeared in a poof of blue smoke, and Azule Linga marched over to the admin building and switched her major from Social Change to Creative Writing, and she never looked back. When she channels the Blue Angel, Azule looks away from the keyboard and lets the keys fall where they may. The Blue Angel's messages are never edited, for the Blue Angel sends electrical impulses from the Blue Light into Azule's typing fingers and thus the messages are flawless: *The Bleu Angle bids us ti embrase the incompresensible in its perefect comprehensibulity.* A shock of white appeared in Azule's long dark wavy hair, right above the spot on her forehead the Blue Angel touched.

Is it possible to have spirituality without narcissism? Isn't it the followers, not the leaders, who are pure—the powerless, wide-eyed, open-hearted lambs willing to abandon all to follow the vision. But these positions are not stable, all organizations have lieutenants and ordained sub-teachers, and in the Middle Ages most groups of zealots eventually went on rampages, bludgeoning and burning and drowning and hanging local clergy Jews landed gentries until armies were raised against them and those who were captured were bludgeoned hung drowned burned alive. The rest fled and gave up the cause or flagellated themselves in secret. Some baptized babies by beating them until they bled and thus became one with Jesus, who wept blood for our sins. Those who weep blood like Jesus are imbued with miraculous powers of healing and eternal life. The poorest of the poor become the chosen people, but can one believe one is chosen without narcissism? No matter how much you deprive yourself of earthly comforts, roaming the countryside in your sackcloth, barefooted, sore-ridden, crazy-eyed. Perhaps it is the sinner who is pure at heart, the drug addict who shares his stash, his brute generosity. The more I look, the more pessimistic I become. Perhaps I'm in the God has abandoned me phase, and when I've reached the pits of utter despair God will give me a vision, and I can go forth and preach my unfettered truth to an aching world.

I stick green tourmaline in my ears to heal my heart. I wear sandalwood around my neck for grounding. I am Azule Linga, Poet of the Blue Light. When I sing the trees listen and the beasts follow. I am the reincarnation of an ancient Jovian saint, a precursor to Buddha. I'm dressed monochromatically in a color with special significance. The senior students who assist me are also dressed monochromatically, but in a lesser color. I begin my discourse with the notion of doubt, and I write on a white board all the negative things people might feel about me. That I'm crazy. That I'm a charlatan. That I'm impossible. Then I peer into your eyes and nod and smile. I know the secret cosmology of the universe, which I am here to share with you. Different planes of reality exist simultaneously, at different levels of vibrations. As you advance spiritually you move through these planes. But how do you advance spiritually? I ask with a twinkle in my eye. It's all about increasing your capacity for love. To get to the fourth level you must attain absolute truthfulness, for truthfulness is a form of love. Truthfulness is the ultimate transmission. When Madonna admitted to peeing while standing in the shower, she was manifesting absolute truth; she was loving her fans. If someone says to you, how are you doing, and you say fine when you're not feeling fine, then you're lying and not loving God. This is all laid out in the sacred *TV Sutras* for those who have advanced high enough to really read them. The fifth level at least. In the beginning, God made all these souls, but they weren't conscious of themselves. The only way to be conscious is to incarnate, and in order to get souls to do that, God in Her infinite wisdom made incarnation an instinct. When voices from other planes speak through people, you shouldn't assume they're telling you the truth, that they know the secrets of the universe. Even if the voices call you "daughter," don't believe them, for they are just as limited and opinionated as you. I was raised in paradise on another planet, but I willingly sacrificed my idyllic life there in order to come to Earth and help a young female victim of child abuse work through her punishing karma, a feat of interplanetary compassion few Earthlings would be capable of. I am always eager to join suffering humanity and bear some of its burdens.

Metaphor: He is a tiger in bed. Metonymy: The tiger called his students to bed.

I think of my Teacher's cock often and completely. His cock is called a lingam, which means wand of light. The Teacher's lingam is too powerful for me to behold on a regular basis; if I were to see too much of it I would die. Thus the Teacher rations his cock, as Jehovah rationed his body with Moses. *And it shall come to pass, while my glory passeth by, that I will put thee in a clift of the rock, and will cover thee with my hand while I pass by: And I will take away mine hand, and thou shalt see my back parts: but my face shall not be seen.* There's a sign-up sheet at the Center, and women who want to sleep with the Teacher add their name to the list. You never know when your name will be called, when you will be chosen. The demand for the Teacher's cock is so high, he penetrates several students a day. A few special women are enlightened enough to behold the wand of light on a regular basis; these are his consorts, and they wield high positions in the cult. Sex is the life force, and fucking is sharing that life force. Women who have blocked energies cannot fully orgasm. The Teacher can release these blockages—he sticks his fingers inside your pussy, places his other hand on your belly and tells you to breathe deeply. The Teacher instructs you to take the energy of his hand into your pussy, to pull that energy up through your body and out the top of your head. Once you can move the Teacher's hand energy you are ready for his cock, and the Teacher then assumes one of eight great coital positions: Most Fierce, Dense Thicket, Dense Blaze, Endowed with Skeletons, Cool Forest, Black Darkness, Resonant with Kilikili, Wild Cries of Ha-ha, or Show Me Your Glory. Even if you've never experienced a vaginal orgasm, you will with the Teacher, and all trauma held in your pussy will be released. The Teacher holds a safe and sacred space at all times. When the Teacher fucks you with his wand of light he clears away all darkness, all limited beliefs, all unhealthy telepathic agreements, and the musty cave of your pussy breaks open to iridescence.

As I perform a Soul dance from Jupiter, dressed in our native white butterfly outfit, I look out the window and all I see are rainbow pastels. When I'm nervous around someone, I lovingly see them as a butterfly flitting about. When doors slam incessantly in a hotel, I see the doors as a line of butterflies flapping their wings. I can sing the Lankavajovian mantra in a resounding high-pitched voice, hardly opening my mouth. Due to its age and heat and high vibrations, diamonds are plentiful on Jupiter. When I was a child we rolled diamonds the size of golf balls across the floor in a game that's a cross between Earth bowling and croquet—except we use our minds to move the balls. On Jupiter our eyes sparkle at the same vibrational frequency as the diamonds, a brightness that would blind a human. Chaos is merely knowledge beyond our conceptual realm. When someone dies the veil of illusion is temporarily rent, and miracles abound. Storm clouds part, a double rainbow gloriously arches above the deceased Teacher's funeral pyre. Corpses smell like flowers. Falling in love and writing can also pierce the veil. I feel things more deeply than ordinary mortals. For instance, if you wanted a banana, I could feel that with my entire body and I would offer you a banana before you could ask for one. I will teach you to alter the face of your art form, to deform the media to say what only you can say. When you're spiritually/creatively/emotionally dead I will bring you back to life. I remember the first time you saw me. You were waiting for class, checking your cellphone. When you looked up, I had arrived. I caught your eye, and you felt recognized, really recognized, like we were old souls reunited. This came as a zap, a jolt—time stood still and there were just the two of us seeing and being seen. Then, bam, the instant passed and I engaged with other students. I can tell you the truth of the universe, I can tell you why you're here, can show you how to activate your molecular crystals, can read your future your palm your aura your heart. Without me you will be a piece of gold undiscovered and covered in dirt. With me there are no more narrative loose ends. I can tell you what became of your junkie neighbor who got evicted, I can tell you where that lost vintage fountain pen went to and what lessons you learned in losing it. I can teach you how to control your subconscious mind. I can reduce your fears and desires to basic bits, like singular musical notes, and I can teach you how to make from them a beautiful song. Thoughts create biochemical reactions in the body. With my techniques we can restore a different biochemical reaction. Bilateral stimulation is key. Together we can cut the past into the future, synthesizing a new text. Repeat after me: *Even though I have this anxiety even though I'm pissed off I'm willing to let it go because it's not serving me right now. I'm ready to let it go. This feeling of rejection. This feeling of abandonment. I've been rejected. I've been abandoned. All this pain. All this hurt. I'm ready to heal. I'm ready to clear this pain. Ready to let go. Clearing it out. Clearing it out. Clearing this pain. Clearing this rejection and abandonment. I may never know why they did or said those things. But I am loveable. I am extremely loveable. I may not show my most loveable side. But I am still loveable.* This is not a religion, it's a philosophy. This is not a religion, it's a science. This is not a religion, it's a toolkit. This is not a religion, it's simply the truth as I know it. Imagine the sense of overwhelm as a wave. Move below and above the wave. See the wave turn translucent, small, eventually a puddle. Step over that puddle into a new state of consciousness. See a turquoise butterfly fluttering about. Sit in a movie theater and watch yourself in a movie. Make it a happy movie, then enter the movie. Continually ask yourself—do I need this right now? When you're willing to let it go, I can channel an ancient sage for you at the introductory rate of $100 an hour. I merely align and allow. Imagine that the difficult person is shrinking to the size of a postage stamp. Imagine that painful memory with circus music playing in the background. Imagine the horrible things she said to you being spoken in the voice of Minnie Mouse. I am a person without fear. My hands are filling with love. I call light and energy from all other realms into present time. The love is free. You've just got to compensate me for my time. $100 an hour and my ancient ancestor will speak through me directly to you. I feel a spinning sensation, then a static electrical charge sparking along my skin, and I am lifted out of the body. In the gleaming black surface of an obsidian mirror I can see beyond your human birth as an Earth child. Abandon selfish action, allow God to use you as it thinks fit. You are an evolution of energy. You are a portal. Open yourself to receive the Blue Light, the Blue Love.

Teachers are used by communities and societies to solve problems that reason and tradition have failed to answer. A Teacher's leadership is a creative, problem-solving strategy that is resorted to in extremis. When it is successful it may be spectacularly so, and give birth to a new civilization or religion. Teachers possess a mysterious presence that others lack. Through them unconscious material emerges into consciousness, rising seemingly out of nowhere to motivate action with a mysterious passion and conviction. Teachers offer a deeply evocative communion, an electrifying blurring of boundaries. Once this communion is experienced and lost, life no longer has its savor, action is no longer potent, and the world becomes colorless and drab. The Teacher's power or talent is often seen as divinely inspired. Part god, part man, the Teacher quests for the secret of eternal life. When a Teacher speaks, the audience listens in breathless suspense. Those who have not heard her speak cannot imagine the power and expressiveness of her language. She transcends genius. The Teacher is utterly fearless. The relationship between him and his followers is one of fealty. The Teacher's lessons are received as a revelation that makes the student feel literally drunk. When the Teacher dies, it's as if the Ten Commandments have suddenly crumbled, and the student keeps a cherished last picture above her desk for forty years. Teachers have an enormous sense of entitlement and they never question their mission. Their childhoods tend to include loss, pressure to excel, sibling rivalries, an absence of an idealizable paternal role model, and a lack of unconditional love. A Teacher is intent upon remaking the world by sheer creative willpower. Her hypnotic appeal is not based on accomplishments or words; it comes from the recognition by the followers of their own lost narcissism, and of the price they have paid for their normality. The Teacher resonates with the followers' unlived lives, evoking an intoxicating yearning for what once was and still might be, and the Teacher does this just through his or her being. "I've become the message now." The Teacher either looks upward to something transcendent or he looks defiantly inward and declares, "I and the Divine are One." His cosmic narcissism is more holistic than the fragmented, separated, ego-driven existences that ordinary people routinely lead, for the Teacher knows no distinction between self and other. The Teacher carefully manages her public displays of emotion, and has an exceptional ability to make whomever she is with feel special. The Teacher is so extraordinary and complete in her ability to be the person that others need her to be, the woman and the mask are one.

I wear pansies on my turban and starbursts on my gown; I glue a jewel to my forehead and swoop into the room, chanting ballads with a brogue. I am a positive being in charge of my own reality, and I share love with all I encounter. People can notice the love. I swirl, lie down on the floor, close my eyes and listen to the language of fairies. I just live my function. I am great and important and marvelous. I am small and petty and personal. I read cards energy bodies auras. Fireworks shoot from my chest. You are not just you; you are also connected to me, a part of me. To make this world different we have to realize that the self is plural. The illusion of the separate self is killing the planet. My body dissolves into rainbow colored radiations, I remain unharmed in fire, walk across water without sinking float a foot above the ground fly across the sky at six hundred leagues a moment, like wind I pass through mountains and rock. My heart is made of love not flesh. During key periods in my life, I have witnessed the dawning of several suns, windows in space, rainbows at night, lights streaming from a corpse, earth tremors, showers of blood, donkeys braying beneath the ground, animals speaking human tongues. Awareness emerges from the darkness of ignorance, a yolk of light—it burns bright for a duration then sinks back into the darkness, then emerges again, an endless flickering cycle. Place the energy of the idea into your heart. Create space. Allow yourself to breathe fully. Allow the process to unfold. Be well. Be happy. Be healthy. Be free. I walk among the ruins scattering white petals of love. My world is perfectly cool and breezy, my breezes blow your sins away. I offer you succor, my moist hair dabbing your sweaty grimy brow. I do not wear a seatbelt because there are no accidents, only errors. Illness is error. If we lived a life free from error we would live forever. There are people out there, agents of error with malicious animal magnetism, who are trying to destroy me. I have a phone installed in my coffin so when I resurrect I can call somebody to get me out of there. Each year students do a soundcheck to make sure the line's still active. I can hold listeners spellbound for hours at a time, speaking with the kind of frenetic pace and energy shared by maniacs and speed freaks. Members commonly leave an all-night session awed by me, but unable to recall the specifics of what I said. They know only that it was incredible, inspirational. Divine. Nectar flows from my nipples. When my nectar impresses your lips, no other Teacher will satisfy you.

The Teacher makes you feel special, singled out. He sits at the front of a packed room full of people, scanning the crowd, and everyone his gaze touches—the lightest of glances—feels chosen. Even though it was I who ended the affair, twenty years later when I find out he slept with all his assistants, I feel betrayed. When you become a student, the energy is so intense you find yourself clinging to every nuance. It's shocking. The power of power. You're sitting in a room with his inner circle and he says your name, and you blush at being singled out. He comes and sits in your two-person breakout group—there are a dozen other groups, many comprised of senior students, but he visits yours. He makes a joke about enlightenment and reaches over and touches your arm. Afterwards during group meditation, you're so obsessing about that touch, it takes ages before you are at all present. As you sit there breathing in synch with the rest of the room, you extend your breath to the guy sitting beside you, and to all the students, especially the ones you don't like, it doesn't matter, you are breathing with them, and then you think of A. and you are breathing with her, and then B. and anybody else you don't like, it doesn't matter, you expand your breathing outward, to the workmen hammering in the distance, to the people in the town, until you are breathing as far as you can imagine, you are breathing with President Obama and Putin, and then your mother and all the dead reaching back through time and when the meditation ends your heart is so open you want to burst, and loving your Teacher feels like the most natural thing, loving anybody, the breathing is love. And then the Teacher says your name. I try not to be negative about him. All the students adored him, set him on a pedestal even though he didn't

claim a pedestal. He's so intelligent and really does pay attention.
Once when I said good-bye to him, he held out his hand to shake—
he was still sitting on the floor—and I leaned down and took his
hand. Later on he told me he used that hand to masturbate with.
Now I'm like—ewe! But in a way, it's marvelously kinky. Why be
so judgmental. It's just energy flying about. Joining any group you
lose yourself—or part of yourself—in the values of that group. If
your life is unbearable—you're alone, you're mourning, you're in
prison, are disconnected, desperate for any reason—those values and
the community they bring with them can offer enormous comfort.
I can't believe how I hooked into him once I was in that student-
Teacher relationship. The structure of it is like a drug.

If you've got your nose inside a Persian rug there is no way you're
going to see a patterning in it. But if you back up, the big picture
emerges. Whether it be masturbating, meditating or eating, I am
100% present. I meet you at a reading, I say something to destabilize
you, I give you a little gift, incense or a crystal. I initiate frequent,
intimate, chaste encounters. Desire sneaks up on you—I am patient,
for I know that moment will come when our little sparks coalesce—
and boom you're throbbing all over the place. I can see things inside
you that no one else can. Follow me and the infinite possibilities of
each moment will be lived fully. You will be greater than Mother
Teresa, but you have to follow me, you have to do everything I tell
you to do. The first step is to allow yourself to experience bliss on a
regular basis. The channel is open. Whatever happens now cannot
be understood with the mind, so don't think about it. Just know that

this is the greatest day of your life. You're special, I tell you over and over. But should you question or disobey me, I shall withdraw, and you will return to the loneliness of the unspecial.

Having arrived early to my chiropractic appointment, I meditate in the car. I hold Kevin's collection of stories *Impossible Princess* against the steering wheel as a prop so that cars trolling for parking spaces will be fooled that I'm sitting there reading, and move on by. Without my glasses the words blur. The longer I stare at the open page, the more I'm able to recognize words through the fuzz; I can't make out individual letters, it's more like I form a psychic connection with the text and the words leap into my brain. It's Kevin's story "Spurt." Book in left hand, propped against the steering wheel, right hand holding lotus seed mala, despite myself, I read: "I helped him insert his big hand through the zipper of my pants." Later: "I've [just?] been to a wake." Words don't come all at once—they pop up individually here and there and eventually a sentence forms. I look like a mannequin, sitting bolt upright. Every passing vehicle I imagine is a cop car, about to pull over and ask, "Ma'am, we've circled around three times, why are you sitting there so freakishly still?" Then the book softens and doubles until its physicality disappears and the after-image of a book floats across the steering wheel. Nobody makes up the original teachings. The teachings sometimes appear in bits and pieces (Joseph Smith with is face in his hat, speaking the words, one by one, as they arise, assistants ready with pen and paper), sometimes fully formed (the Tibetan who writes out the terton he's discovered in its entirety, twice, in order to validate it)—the teaching is delivered to the world and believers coalesce around it—a sticky tar baby. Once when I parodied sheeplike followers, my Buddhist Teacher lover asked, "What about the beauty of belief?" This is the one true thing he ever said to me. Beliefs should not be judged as true or false or ludicrous or reasonable. Beliefs should be judged like art or women or sunsets—by their beauty, by the x-factor that makes us fall in love with them. Belief should spasm our hearts with desire.

A bright beam of light comes down from above and enters my body through the top of my head. The light shines out through my eyes, ears, nose, mouth, cunt, anus and pee hole—each pore of my skin emits a ray of white light so that I look like a porcupine covered in quills of light. In the middle of a blizzard I can raise my body temperature eighteen degrees through the power of concentration alone, I can dry wet sheets draped over my shoulders. I live on a twelve-foot-high wooden platform and wear no clothes. A barricade of wooden planks hides my naked body from my devotees. I see the true reality behind the fascia of language. I bless devotees by touching their heads with my foot and heal the infirm just by looking at them. I was born near a large body of water, where spirit entered into the womb of a virgin, the queen of heaven. I have the ability to stay underwater for thirty minutes at a time, without resurfacing for air. I control wild animals and tell the future. I sleep only three hours each night and can roll around in fire for up to ten minutes, protected only by a thin wool shawl, which has tested negative for fire retardant. I have levitated into the air for four minutes in front of a crowd of 150 witnesses. I can slow my heart and pulse to nearly zero, can perspire from my forehead upon command in my freezing Himalayan retreat, can regurgitate at will to cleanse myself. I exhibit progressive and spectacular modifications in my EEG records during my deepest meditations, including recurrent beta rhythms of 18-20 cycles per second in the Rolandic area of my brain, a generalized fast activity of small amplitude as high as 40-45 cycles per second with occasional amplitudes reaching 30 to 50 microvolts, and the reappearance of slower alpha waves after Samadhi, or ecstasy, has ended. I exhibit no alpha-wave blocking when I'm bombarded with loud banging, strong lights, and other sensory stimuli, and I show persistent alpha activity while holding my hands in ice-cold water for forty-five to fifty-five minutes. I once sat cross-legged in a subterranean 216-cubic-foot cubicle and remained there for sixty-two hours. I once was confined for nine hours in a pit some two by three by four feet, that was covered with wire meshing, a rubber sheet, and cotton carpet. There I maintained the shavasana, or corpse pose, using ujjayi breathing while remembering the names of God. When I was released from the pit, I immediately walked about the grounds and demonstrated athletic feats including a headstand with my legs in the lotus position. When I was a student, I stood in the doorway of an autopsy room and nearly passed out from the stench. I felt myself not wanting to enter, but I forced myself. Inside was a bloated corpse that had been found in a canal. Worms were crawling in it. When I looked up at the ceiling, I could see where previous corpses had exploded and guts had gone flying. My first thought was Let me out of here! But I stayed with it, the corpse and my aversion. As I became accustomed to the odor, I hardly noticed it. I felt honored to see a human corpse in that state, hideous and grotesque. Observing the colors and the maggots and the worms, I began to find it quite beautiful. I have wild, waistlong hair and a nose ring. I dress in red. I have survived without food for seventy years. I meditate to get energy. By studying me, mankind will better be able to work out strategies for survival during natural calamities, extreme conditions, and extra-terrestrial explorations to the Moon and Mars. I was blessed by a goddess when I was aged eight, which has enabled me to survive without sustenance. Each time I breathe in, all the stars and planets are drawn into me and when I breathe out they're expelled back into black sky.

There are three types of revealed teachings: earth treasures, intention treasures, and TV treasures. Earth treasures include not only texts, but also sacred images, ritual instruments, and medicinal substances, and are found in many places: temples, monuments, statues, mountains, rocks, trees, lakes, and even the sky. An intention treasure appears directly within the mind of the recipient in the form of sounds or letters. The intention treasure is received during meditation. A TV treasure is buried in an ordinary television broadcast. The TV treasure potential has previously been implanted in the mind of the receiver, via direct transmission from a powerful Teacher, either in a past life or the present incarnation. At a beneficent time, the TV treasure is transmitted to the receiver via light beams and broadcast sound which activate the eyes and the ears. Simultaneously, the meaning of the transmission appears whole and complete in the mind of the receiver. The receiver must remain sitting cross-legged before the television and copy down the text and its commentary, exactly as it was received, in a spiral bound journal. A TV treasure is so powerful, no test of authenticity is required. I write this in the nude, ectoplasm streaming from my vagina.

While fucking a student, the Teacher is struck by how surprisingly empty sex can be. All these desperate women, he thinks—it's like shooting ducks in a pond. Later that day a student is informed that her sister has been killed in a car accident. He makes her tea and holds her as she weeps. They're like animals, sitting there in each other's arms, wrapped in the clean energy of inconsolable grief. The light flickers through the lush foliage outside the lodge's window. Her fleshy warmth trembling with tears, her total trust, her body clinging to his, all pretense, all bullshit dropped—the duck is irresistible. She needs to leave for a few days, so he begins emailing her. "You seem strangely familiar," he writes.

I dream my skin is soft because it's been pummeled by meteorites.

In the cult I tried to raise my vibrations high enough to visit the inner temples where all knowledge, past and future, is stored—but I failed. I was a twenty-something lesbian in Indiana who longed to be a spiritual poet, which meant I wrote clichéd abstractions and forced similes to suggest I was a deep person. I was high on spirituality. Those moments when we were struck with the acute awesomeness of existence, Nance and I called epiphanies. The cult never used the word epiphany; I learned it in a comp lit class when we read Joyce's *Dubliners*. Epiphanies were so common in our lives, we chuckled about them, discussed them with the casual enthusiasm we used for David Bowie or our latest granola recipe. I keep returning to one afternoon at the park. Nance and I loved to play on the swing set, pumping our legs in unison and whooshing back and forth with abandon. I remember sitting there afterwards, our feet digging into the sandpit, swaying and lightly twirling from the chains that held our seats, when suddenly perception shifted, crystallized. My heart and eyes twirled open, the world *trees sky grass robins Bloomington houses with their ubiquitous large front porches the bluebird that attacked my head whenever I entered my frontyard dirt roar of car engines sickeningly sweet jasmine comparative literature Nance* was impossibly bright and vast and I was at the center of it all, ravenous with life. "Do you feel it," I said to her. "Uh huh." No one told me that moving closer into what I perceived on a daily basis, the swingness of the swing, was the key to spiritual writing. In the cult the goal was to transcend this lower self and connect to higher levels. Our epiphanous mode was almost too effortless to call profound. It was like we'd discovered a new taste that those dreary non-cult others couldn't—or wouldn't—open their mouths to, the way my mother grimaced at fresh mushrooms. Perhaps what we were feeling was simply our youth. Life still felt endless, a new excitement waiting for us around every corner. I loved people back then, loved talking, feeling a lover's heat waft through the illusion of space and into my heart.

As I walk down 3rd Street on a Friday afternoon, blue pops out— blue doors, blue signs, billboards, flags, people rush towards me in bright blue jackets, people with bright blue bags, hats, umbrellas, bicycles, a scarf the same periwinkle as the sweater my mother wore in her coffin, blue cars jump into the act—so much blue assaults me it's frightening, like a Japanese ghost movie where the blue guy rushing towards me's eyes grow blankly intense and he shoots me a meaningful glare, but then I realize his eyes are mere windshields and someone or something else is riding around inside his blue-hooded skull, peering out, something so foreign, so other that the very notion of meaning shatters. Blue has disturbed the random order of daily encounter, blue, my mother's favorite color, and I'm certain it's *her* presence wafting from this monochromatic excess. The sutra I received on the anniversary of her death: #71: *Proof—apparitions, hard-core voice phenomena—and we're going to get it.* The only sutra referencing the otherworld; the azure sky is so vast and vivid my eyes tear. I board the Mission bus and take the only seat available, beside an old guy who smells of alcohol. He starts talking to me but I can't understand him, he keeps saying over and over something that sounds like "ah-lemony." Then the woman on the other side of me speaks to him in Spanish, and I hear "ah-lemony" again. The woman says to me, "You don't know 'ah-lemony'?" I say no, and she looks confused and surprised, the way I do when I awaken from a dream and bring back a nonsense word or some great line of poetry that makes no sense in the waking world. It is at this point that I notice how the other passengers are filled with life, I see it racing beneath their skin, like vampires can in the movies. *Ah-lemony* is the sutra of the day. And what commentary arises? Sutras are a process, not a fossil. Each day, each moment the world offers new sutras for those tuned in to listen. No Truth, just passing bleeps of meaning, kiss them lightly then let them go. Sutra 78: *It's personal management. The key word is personal.* On the TV Woody Allen and Mia Farrow, dressed as a trashy woman with huge breasts, walk through a park, talking. She tells him she isn't attracted to handsome men, that she goes for intellectuals. In my notebook I write: *Structures are helpful, but in the end you need to carve out your own path.* That's it, I think, shouldn't the commentary to the final sutra be more grandiose? So I keep sitting there squinting my brain for inspiration when the door buzzer shatters the calm. I slam my notebook shut and run down the stairs to sign for some packages.

As part of my duties, I go up to the third floor of the compound to lay out the Teacher's futon. He's in the office next to the bedroom, wearing long underpants and a crepe shirt. He's writing something. I say, "Please pardon my intrusion." I'm slouched over the futon, spreading out the sheets when my Teacher suddenly leans against me from behind. This happens in the blink of an eye. While pushing down on me, my Teacher pulls at the collar of my blouse. The buttons pop off and scatter about. I desperately try to flee, but with my Teacher's enormous body crushing me, I'm unable to move. He tears open my skirt, panting harshly, and shoves his hand into my panties. I'm so afraid I'm unable to speak. Then my Teacher spears me from behind. As I struggle and writhe, everything goes pitch black. How much time elapses, I have no idea. Though I was prostrate when I blacked out, when I regain consciousness I'm lying under the blankets facing the ceiling. It's low and covered with perforated white acoustical tiles. I'm petrified with terror, but somehow manage to roll onto the floor. Clutching my clothes, I crawl away, but the Teacher yanks on my ankle and shouts, "Let's stay in bed awhile!" I keep crawling and he keeps yanking and I keep crawling and I make it to the door, heart beating frantically. I bang my knee on the threshold and hit my head on the frame. My Teacher is still pursuing me, and I run down to the second floor and dash into the bathroom. Violent nausea overtakes me. Over and over I wipe at the body fluids which smear my lower parts. Even after my skin turns red, I continue wiping. That night during satsang, I feel the Teacher's eyes boring into me. He says, "There are two types of mentalities, that of the fly, and that of the bee. The fly looks for the toxins and the bee for the nectar. Which would you rather meditate on, toxins or nectar?"

Dampness inside my nostrils, inrush of cool air disturbing that dampness. I worry about the plainness of my writing, my stupidity, lack of depth. Is there such a thing as depth—or is there simply staring and staring until things shift and a teeny chink opens to you. Do I know any more now than when I was a child lying on my back, gazing out at the vast night sky, overcome with awe, wondering if the universe was limited or limitless—either way I knew I was fucked, a mere bleep. I am no philosopher or spiritual know-it-all. I have no training, no inherent—or inherited—right to be writing this, here on my bed holding my midnight blue fountain pen, surrounded by three cats—Quincey to my left, Ted to my right licking his back leg, Sylvia on the air filter across the room because she's avoiding Quincey. Space heater is on, door is closed, we're cozy on this brisk winter day.

The preciseness of this specific moment—red cotton plush throw on my legs—pink chenille bathrobe on arms and chest, visible as I look at the page—matters—in the backlighting from the window, the highlights on Sylvia's fur glow—I fear that *The TV Sutras* is jejune, has been said a zillion times over. But that's the point—not only is there no definitive truth, realization comes in flashes, like a match blasting into life, then fading. It doesn't last, it happens over and over again, from person to person. Tarting up the text and calling my experience of this moment "empathetic intersubjective consciousness" does not get to any sort of core awareness—it speaks to the professionalization that's overtaken the world—we need advanced degrees, specialized vocabularies to hide the sad fact that what we're saying is obvious and not necessarily experiential, that some near-illiterate Christian mother in the boonies may "know" more about the nature of reality than we do. Sylvia is now sitting on my left thigh, journal on right thigh; because of this my writing is cramped. Ted is rolling on his back, pink belly showing through short white hair growing back from when he was shaved for his operation. I pile moment upon moment upon moment, determined to capture the present, as if that would say something important—but the harder I try to grasp the now, the further it recedes, buried in other presents that bleed into this one, muddied by the dogma from all the cults I belong to—the cult of experimental writing, the cult of those who carry backpacks instead of briefcases to work, of adjunct creative writing instructor; the cult of radical queerness, of San Francisco, of California, of the United States of America; the cult of the female body, the cult of global warming, virulent capitalism, confused vegetarianism; the cult of consumerism, of New Age autodidacticism; the cult of aging, of terror of time running out. Sometimes I belong to the cult of monogamy, sometimes not. I pile moment upon moment. No singularity, no verdicts, only chords and this endless accrual.

The densest molecule is the diamond molecule; if one of its atoms were blown up to the size of an orange, the space between it and the next atom would be two football fields away. Space defines matter and nothing ever touches. You have an infinite amount of divisions within yourself. It's all dots inside of dots inside of dots, surrounded by endless space. Even during sex, there is a vast space between your dots and your lover's dots; you can never really touch another's skin, only aquaplane above it. Spacetime is infinitely divisible and the vacuum flows in spiral fashion toward singularity. Gravity is the vacuum descending to greater and greater complexity, at the "bottom" of which is consciousness itself. The material world is a teeny leak of the vacuum. Protons spin near the speed of light and thus you are light, a galaxy of mini black holes spinning. That's how energetic you are. Energy is spinning within my cells my atoms my protons my god particles, I'm strobing towards you, a smattering of matter in an infinity of dense space flickering in and out of existence being non-being being, my love reaching out of the darkness, so bright it blinds; eternity is now and in San Francisco. Receding into the distance, a blonde-headed woman sweeps the temple floor and bows. I have the heart of Buddha, the compassion of Jesus Christ, the fire of Shakti, the wisdom of Quan Yin. I am the priestess of

Ganymede, my pyramid-shaped atoms twirling through dense space; I am the love child of blue-eyed Atlanteans and highly-evolved beings from the constellation Orion. The blueprint of the universe is an isotropic vector matrix and I have attained vector equilibrium. I am a fractal hallucinating reality, the vacuum surrounding me feeding information inward, my bits of matter feeding information outward—I am a spinning cocreator. I will never die.

ACKNOWLEDGMENTS

Sutras 1-16 were published in *2nd Avenue Poetry,* Volume 3: Occult, 2010 (2ndavepoetry.com/2ndAve_3/v3dodiebellamy.html).

The *TV Sutras* (without description or commentary) were exhibited with photographs by Colter Jacobsen, as part of SF Camerawork's group show *As Yet Untitled: Artists & Writers in Collaboration,* January 6th–April 16th, 2011.

Thanks to Ed Sanders for permission to print his poem. Thanks to Neil LeDoux for his amazing illustrations; to Kevin Killian for editorial advice and handholding and love; to Steve Seidenberg for his generous read and eagle eye; to Ugly Duckling Presse and to Anna Moschovakis for being the bestest (and most patient) editor imaginable.